ZEN

THE SUPREME EXPERIENCE

THE NEWLY DISCOVERED SCRIPTS

ZEN

THE SUPREME EXPERIENCE

THE NEWLY DISCOVERED SCRIPTS

ALAN WATTS

EDITED BY MARK WATTS

vega

To Michael Wenger at the San Francisco Zen Center

© Vega 2002
Text copyright © Alan Watts 2002

UK ISBN 1 84333 614 6
US ISBN 1 84333 714 2

A CIP catalogue record for this book is available from the British Library

First published in the UK in 2002 by Vega
64 Brewery Road, London N7 9NT

A member of **Chrysalis** Books plc

Visit our website at www.chrysalisbooks.co.uk

Editorial: Richard Emerson, Lydia Darbyshire, Mike Flynn
Design: Justina Leitão
Production: Susan Sutterby
Project management: Anna Ludlow
Indexing: Indexing Specialists

Printed and bound in Slovenia

CONTENTS

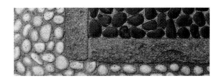

DURING THE FIFTIES AND SIXTIES, Alan Watts made his mark as one of the foremost authorities on Eastern spiritual belief lecturing in the West and, most importantly, as the person credited with introducing Zen Buddhism to the USA. He expounded on his subject through countless radio talks, lectures, books and articles, bringing the thoughts and works of Eastern scholars to a wider audience, first in America and, later, Europe.

As a master of both the spoken and written word, Alan Watts' boundless enthusiasm for his subject has kept audiences enthralled throughout the world, while his encyclopedic and insightful knowledge has both informed and motivated all those who have attended his lectures and discussions. Alan died in 1973 but his son, Mark, is continuing his father's vocation through the Alan Watts foundation, bringing Zen Buddhism to a new generation of readers, listeners and supporters.

Much of Alan Watts' work has already been published, but some of his early taped lectures lay almost forgotten in a cupboard for many years and have only recently resurfaced. Transcripts of those rediscovered lectures, edited and adapted by Mark Watts, along with other writings by Alan Watts that have never previously been published in printed form, have been brought together in this new anthology, called *Zen – The Supreme Experience*. With the exception of two chapters – Just So – I and II – all parts of this book stand alone and so can be read in any order, consecutively or individually, as the reader chooses. Nevertheless, collectively they provide an important insight into the mysterious world of Zen and a unique glimpse into the mind of probably the Western world's greatest interpreter of Eastern spiritual thought.

Throughout this book you will find photographs and illustrations designed to set the mood and to highlight key parts of the text. Many pages also feature quotations taken from the Tao-te Ching and other famous works by the Zen masters that have inspired Alan Watts and countless others before him and since.

To set the scene, this anthology includes a foreword by Mark Watts, who talks about his father and explains how this latest work came into being. The introduction is by Alan Watts himself, the text drawn from one of his previously unpublished talks.

PREFACE

THE RECORDINGS UPON WHICH this work is based lay in a closet for forty years, untouched and all but forgotten. Quite recently Charlotte Selver, the legendary founder of the Sensory Awareness Movement, rediscovered the tapes. For those of you who may be unfamiliar with the life of my father or his prolific works, a few words should be said to place him and this remarkable series of lectures given in New York in 1958 into context.

Alan Watts was born near London in 1915. His father was a representative of the Michelin Tyre Company, and his mother was an instructor at a boarding school for the daughters of Christian missionaries travelling abroad. The missionaries would often return from the Far East with gifts of landscape miniatures and finely embroidered fabrics with religious motifs. Alan was fascinated by images of Taoist monks wandering in the vast mountains and by the strange icons of exotic religions.

As a consequence of this early exposure to Eastern art, years later, while attending King's School in Canterbury, he took a keen interest in the cultures of China and Japan. Eventually he also discovered a local bookstore specializing in philosophical works, including publications from the Buddhist Lodge in London. He soon introduced himself at the lodge where he met the famous Buddhist lawyer Christmas 'Toby' Humphries, and not long afterward the Zen Buddhist scholar D.T. Suzuki came to speak.

THE MIDDLE WAY

Within a few years, Alan had became the editor of *The Middle Way*, the journal that had originally led him to the Lodge, and was delivering lectures on Taoism, and Chan and Zen Buddhism. In 1936 at the age of 21, he published the first of his many books, *The Spirit of Zen*, and a few years later he moved to New York.

There he studied Zen practice very briefly, but due to a lack of career opportunities in the field he joined the seminary, became an episcopal priest, and served as chaplain at Northwestern University. However, he resigned from the Church in 1950 to pursue what would prove to be a lifelong study of the philosophies of Asia.

After leaving the Church in 1950, Alan returned to New York where he met

FOREWORD

Joseph Campbell, Luisa Coomaraswamy, and *avant-garde* composer John Cage. He then received an invitation from Fredric Spiegelberg to come to San Francisco to teach at the Academy of Asian Studies in San Francisco, and in late 1950 moved west with his young wife, Dorothy.

They lived in Palo Alto where they had the first of five children before moving across the Golden Gate to the woodsy suburbs of Main County, and bought a small home. By then Alan had become Dean of the Academy, and with more children on the way settled into the life as a writer. Not long afterwards he resumed his public lectures, upon which the current work is based.

NARRATIVE SKILLS

Growing up with Alan Watts as our father we became aware of his narrative skills at a very young age. The high point of each day arrived just before bedtime when we were treated to the adventures of Thud and Zudd, two wise rabbits who each evening outwitted weasels and buzzards before taking refuge in their labyrinth of tunnels.

When occasionally he would grow tired of inventing new episodes for the imaginary rabbits he would turn to Hindu mythology, and we would sit spellbound by images of a sleeping god who dreamed

the world into being, all the time playing a cosmic game of hide and seek by pretending not to know himself.

Of course, every few million years or so, the sleeping god would awaken to knowledge of who he was, and play with his brothers and sisters as we played among the pines in the yard. Yet all this took place in another world in a distant galaxy, or perhaps inside a speck of dust on a nearby phonograph turntable cover.

During this period in the mid-fifties, while Alan was the Dean at the Academy, bedtime stories were occasionally replaced by evenings spent at the Academy, where he would speak to a room full of students, faculty and friends about the philosophies of the Far East.

At the time, he was also working on a manuscript that would become *The Way of Zen* on a Bollingen grant arranged by Joseph Campbell, and so his talks generally centred around Zen themes. The evening talks were well attended, and soon led to other local speaking engagements and eventually to a public radio show.

THE EARLY RECORDINGS

As far as we know, his academy talks were never recorded since portable tape decks were rare at that time, and until recently it was thought that the earliest Watts recording had been made years later during his regular Saturday evening sessions at KPFA, in Berkeley, California.

In preparation for an early Sunday morning broadcast, Alan would go into the broadcasting booth each Saturday evening and record 28 minutes and 30 seconds on a previously announced topic. The first of these recordings was a series on 'The Great Books of Asia', soon followed by a popular season of talks entitled 'Way Beyond the West'.

Lacking a live audience and given the rigid format, his early radio lectures tended to be formal and decidedly scholarly in tone compared to his longer and more humorous Academy talks. Still, the radio series proved to be immensely popular, and some of the talks were aired on KPFK in Los Angeles as well as other radio affiliates in Portland, Dallas. Eventually the major public stations in Boston and New York began to broadcast the series as well.

LIVE TALKS

By 1962, the studio recordings had given way to live talks as Alan began to be recorded on a regular basis, often by his future archivist, Henry Jacobs. Over the years, an extensive collection of recordings was amassed, and in the early seventies, the Electronic University began offering courses on cassette from the library. However, few of the early recordings were included owing to the contrast between his early radio style and his fluid later talks.

ENTHUSIASM AND HUMOUR

With the discovery of the late fifties Zen tapes the spontaneous and vital tone of his early public talks was also rediscovered, and reveal the enthusiasm and humour with which he approached his subject. Although he touches briefly on the history of Zen, it is the experience of Zen that takes centre stage as we follow him through New York in the spring of 1958.

To round out the work, a few talks from a seminar, 'The World as Just So', have been integrated within the later chapters as well, adding a seasoned flavour reflective of his mature works, and taken together offer a most vital perspective of the world of Zen.

Mark Watts

I MUST BEGIN WITH A WORD of explanation. Some time ago I was in a radio station as a participant in a panel discussion on man and religion. Before we went on air, the moderator asked all the participants around the table to introduce themselves. I was sitting on his left, and the man on his right began: Rabbi So-and-so, Jewish; Reverend So-and-so, Protestant minister; Father So-and-so, Catholic priest; Doctor So-and-so, professor of philosophy, logical positivist and so on. When it was my turn, I said, 'Alan Watts, no label.' Immediately there was an outcry: 'You aren't being fair.'

I say 'No label' sincerely, because although I speak a great deal about Zen, I never refer to myself as a 'Zen-ist' or as a Buddhist because that seems to me like packaging the sky.

There is an excellent reason for the absence of a definition of Zen. All systems that have preconceived views of what the human being is and what the world ought to be categorize existence under labels. People who have Jehovah-like ideas of an order that they wish to impose on reality also use labels. But when one's concern is not to order the world around but to understand it, to experience it and to find it out about it, you give up this superior attitude and become receptive.

Then, instead of knowing all about it, you come to know it directly. But this 'knowing' is difficult to talk about because it has to be felt. It is the difference between eating dinner and eating the menu. Eating dinner is the expression of Zen and of Taoism through one's whole organism, and the awareness of the organism in this integral relationship is essential to Zen and to Taoism.

It is important that we use the word 'organism' in this context rather than the word 'body', 'physical apparatus' or any such term. Because the view of the universe that originated with Taoism – and was later imparted to Zen – is an organic view of the world, we must pause at the start to find out what that means. We need to define 'organism' by differentiating it from a 'mechanism'. A mechanism is always constructed by taking separate parts and assembling them in accordance with a preconceived order. The assembly of a mechanism requires, in the first place, someone (external to the organization of the mechanism) to put it together, someone with a preconceived plan of what it ought to be. An organism is operationally, functionally different. It does not begin as an assemblage of parts but as a more or less simple structure that, as it grows, constellates its parts out of itself, from within, working outwards. It begins as a whole, and it ends as a whole. It is not constructed. In a funny way, all the parts happen altogether simultaneously. There doesn't seem to be a controlling agent.

An old Chinese parable tells of a body whose active, busy members began to complain about the stomach. The hands, feet and all-knowing head got together and said: 'Stomach gets all the food but doesn't do any work. We eyes, we see; we show how to get around. We feet, we carry. We hands, we even go so far as to lift this lazy stomach's food to the mouth. We've had enough of this, and we are going on strike. We're not going to feed the stomach any more.' Well, you know what happened: they all got weaker and weaker and began to lose their power. In the human being — the totality of the human organism — we must consider all the major parts as equals, each playing a necessary role for the welfare of the whole.

Still we Westerners wonder how on earth anything manages to keep from going hopelessly amok if there isn't someone in charge. We even think this in the United States, where we call our society a democracy.

CONSTRUCTING THE UNIVERSE
We think this way because we have inherited a cultural tradition that tends to look on the universe as a mechanism constructed by a divine architect who had in his mind the logos, the plan, the order, before he constructed the artefact. And we perceive his creation to be a realization of the divine plan of the logos in psychophysical terms.

We look on our universe, then, as a construct, something that has been made. Even when we are atheist or agnostic and believe in scientific empiricism, we still continue this pattern of thought because we understand our universe in mechanical terms — constructing, intellectual, mathematical. Since we represent the world of nature in these terms, we get confused and begin to think that the terms themselves are the very nature of the reality being represented — as if in translating colour, music, taste and touch into words we become convinced that these were simply nothing but noise. With this background, it's a bit difficult for us to begin to appreciate how there can be order in this world if there is no controlling agent or mechanical structure.

Yet this is the fundamental Taoist conception of nature, which is called *tzu-jan* ('self-so') — everything functioning by itself, spontaneously. Everything is mutually arising, not something first and then something second. Not darkness first, then light. Not one end of things first and then another, but somehow everything coming into being together. This is the fundamental Taoist conception of the nature of the world and the various contrary or correlative aspects of it, the prototypes that are, in Chinese, *yang* (the positive principle) and *yin* (the negative principle). *Yang*, being the masculine and *yin*, the feminine. These concepts do not have superior or inferior connotations. The male is not superior, nor is the female inferior. They arise mutually. There is no meaning to *yang* without *yin*, and no meaning to *yin* without *yang*. Take away *yang* and there is no *yin*. Take away *yin* and there is no *yang*.

If we consider a multiplicity of events or things or facts as constituting the world, we can logically understand that there must always have been at least two of them. One thing alone, one fact alone, one event alone is utterly inconceivable. You couldn't recognize it – it would be like seeing a black cat on a dark night, an unrecognizable darkness, since there would be no light in which to contrast the shapes. It would look very much as your head looks to your eyes without the aid of a mirror.

If we can see that we live in an organic world that functions *tzu-jan* – of itself – in order to be lived harmoniously, this world must not be treated as something to be bossed around or, in other words, to be subject to our will. Fundamental to Taoist philosophy is the attitude called *wu-wei* (the Japanese say *mui*), meaning 'non-interference', 'non-striving', 'non-pushing' – not mere inactivity. One of the most marvellous illustrations of *wu-wei* is jujitsu (or judo), a very active martial art. But you do not oppose your opponent. You take him as he comes and lead him to his logical conclusion. In fact, jujitsu is a practical application of Taoist philosophy. So we are not talking in this respect about a 'relaxed' attitude to life as the word is currently misused.

RELAXING

Many people think that to be relaxed is to be like a damp cloth on a clothes line. The key to relaxation in Taoist thinking is balance – the harmonious balance of *yang* and *yin*. When one moves an arm, for example, what happens? When we flex our muscles this way, the biceps contract and the triceps relax. It is a relaxed movement, even though it involves both relaxation and tension, both *yin* and *yang*. Oddly enough, in our medical nomenclature, the biceps and triceps are called 'antagonistic' muscles, whereas they should be called 'complementary' muscles. If we make them fight, we get paralysed. The Taoist would make the point that paralysis is inevitably the result of taking a 'God Almighty' attitude towards the universe. In the Tao-te Ching, Lao-tzu says:

The great Tao flows everywhere,
    both to the left and to the right.
By it all things come into being
    and nothing is rejected.
It loves and nourishes all things,
    but does not lord it over them.
Merits accomplished, it lays no claim to them.

Instead of controlling events it acts like the judo principle, like water. We might almost say 'it stoops to conquer', but 'conquering' is not the right word; it collaborates, rather. The Tao-te Ching was written as a book of advice for rulers, and many of its chapters advise the emperor how to conduct himself. A delightful saying is: 'Govern a great state as you would call a small fish. Do it gently.' Another is: 'When I see a man take the empire in hand, I know there will be no end to it.' Lao-tzu is warning the ruler that if he alters something that looks as if it ought to be put right, two other things will go out of kilter; they will have lost their adjustments, and he has to move quickly to correct them. But that means he will also have to alter this... and this... and this...

Our world is complicated today because we take a 'God Almighty' attitude and have to control every detail. Yet as an organism, we came into being without our conscious interference and with a very small amount of co-operation on the part of our parents. We happened without being directed; we grew in the womb. The food our mother ate was transmuted, in a process quite unknown to her, into nourishment for us. This elaborate and marvellous structure, intricately ordered, came into being without our knowing how we did it.

The whole philosophy of Taoism, its wisdom about the nature of humans, is based on watching, on observation. Yet this observing is not what most people think of when told, 'Pay attention, be aware'. What happens in school when our teachers want us to pay attention? There are a few clever teachers who never tell us to pay attention because they are fascinating. Usually, though, when she sees a child's attention wandering, the teacher raps the desk and says, 'Pay attention!' She has an insecure feeling that if all eyes in the class are not looking in her direction, the pupils' minds must be wandering. If she sees children doodling on their pads and looking through the window or twiddling their thumbs she is sure their minds are not with her. The children, of course, know what she wants to see. She wants to see them frowning and staring, wrapping their legs tightly around the legs of the chair so that, holding on, they are quite sure they are conscious and concentrating. So we learn that the mechanism of attention, of awareness, is a muscular undertaking, which is forced on to the object of our concentration.

CONCENTRATING

When Western people first study Oriental philosophy or start practising yoga they learn that the essential prerequisite is concentration. They give themselves headaches by staring at buttons and so on. When they find their attention wandering, they say, 'Naughty, naughty! Come back to the point.' And all of it is like smoothing waves of water with an iron. This imperious state of mind – the attitude that says, 'Don't wander' – is not what is meant by *huan*, the Chinese term for the kind of contemplation, or watching, I'm talking about. To be aware is the natural state of one's nervous system, of one's senses, of one's mind (whatever that may be). It does it all by itself, spontaneously (*tzu-jan*), just as your stomach digests food by itself, your eyes receive light, your tongue tastes and your ears hear sounds.

If you want to be aware of something, all you have to do is to look at it. It requires no muscle strain, no gritting of the teeth – just a simple assumption that something put in front of your mind, or your mind's eye, will stay there until moved. And it will stay, if you are not trying to force it. This basic attitude is the source of Taoist wisdom about the nature of the individual. When we observe these goings-on, we begin to learn that our organism is not only sufficiently intelligent to have constructed itself but also smart enough to do almost everything necessary to function and adapt to its environment.

That is to say, we know very well that if we get cut, various healing processes immediately go to work to get rid of infection. When infected, our temperature rises in order to boil the bugs out of our blood. In the days when medicine considered fever to be an illness and tried to rid the body of fever, the treatment often ended up killing the patient. We learned later in medicine to trust the fever and co-operate with it.

This attitude, of course, does not mean that we leave everything up to the organism inside its skin. We can also help by making certain motions outside the skin, as long as we co-operate with what is already going on inside. And just as our temperature rises to boil out the bugs, so it goes with the play of our feelings; they, too, are a kind of homeostatic self-adjusting process.

FEELING

We are often tyrannical about the way we feel. We are taught that there are 'good' feelings and 'bad' feelings. If we are depressed, this is a bad feeling; we should do something about it. Anger is also a bad feeling that we should fix, because we are afraid that if we let ourselves be angry we will punch someone in the nose. This is because we really know nothing about our feelings. We have never had this attitude of *huan* ('aware contemplation') towards them.

Take the previous example: 'I feel furious.' If I say 'naughty, naughty' and sit on the fury, it may go away, but, as we know, it will emerge elsewhere unconsciously, making us intolerable to our friends in a manner of which we ourselves are unaware. It's tricky. Another quick way of getting rid of anger (because we can't take it) is to hit someone on the jaw. That dissipates the anger. It is something quite different to watch the feeling and see what it truly is. We get this hot-under-the-collar feeling and quickly jump to the conclusion that it is anger. How do you know it is anger? Why not watch it to see what it really is instead of knowing how to classify it? Let's observe this oily sensation inside us, say, and see what it wants to do. You never know – if you watch, it may boil and boil and then stop boiling. And that will be that. And you'll feel better, because your feelings are an ingenious process of adaptation – a stream of sensations, of psychological adjustment.

BREATHING AND QUIETING

Now I want to speak particularly of the Taoist attitude towards two fundamental processes of the organism, breath and sexuality, which are central to what we might call the Taoist style of yoga. All schools of yoga involve breathing, but they take many different approaches to it. We should also clarify what meditation is from a Taoist and a Soto Zen point of view. *Zazen* – Zen sitting meditation – is simply the proper way to sit. To construe it as an exercise is against the spirit of Zen, because exercises are manipulative processes through which you ready yourself for something. In *zazen* there is no particular thing to get ready for. We have it now. There is no need for preparation.

Buddhism speaks, for example, of the four fundamental attitudes of man, which they call the 'Four Dignities': walking, standing, sitting and lying. To practise Zen correctly is to do every one of them *à la* Zen. Sitting is what you do when you have nothing else to do. When you quite naturally sit at rest after being busy, why must you do anything else? Must one improve one's mind? Can't we just sit down? Must we be busy even when we sit? Must we justify this waste of time by treating it as a spiritual exercise?

No. The attitude here is that it is not a spiritual exercise; it has no purpose except sitting merely to sit. So all compulsive practice of *zazen* and yoga and whatnot – thinking one is going to catch some animal called *satori*

('enlightenment') – is fundamentally off the point as far as this philosophical point of view is concerned. There is no purpose, no goal to be attained from sitting except sitting. When you sit down you don't practise making yourself like a log, you don't try vigorously to wipe every impression out of your mind, for that again is smoothing rough waters with an iron. You just let whatever is happening happen. The street sounds of vehicles, of dogs barking, of people grunting and feet shuffling – all these things go through your mind like sounds in a hollow room, like birds going through the sky, leaving no particular tracks. You become aware of what your body is doing.

The most obvious thing about your body is the rhythm of its breath, and you will notice funny things about breathing. You will notice that the way you breathe reveals a great deal about your basic attitude. The 'clutching' type of personality – which most of us have – breathes in a clutching way, retentively, as if it were unwilling to let go of valuable air because it is the breath of life. In this Taoist yoga you don't say, 'My breathing is clutching and therefore must become relaxed.' That would make an exercise out of it. You simply watch what your breathing is doing, without interfering. Eventually, because it is being allowed to be itself, the breath gets quieter. It automatically adjusts. It becomes smoother, and in the end it becomes so quiet that it seems as if there is no breathing at all.

Some schools of Taoist (and Indian) yoga say that the object of breathing practice is to stop the breath. In other words, the practice is a kind of marathon to see how long you can hold your breath until you eventually break the record. That simply is not the point. To stop the breath is to go against the first principle of Taoism, *wu-wei* ('let go'). So the quietness, the non-breathing is simply a metaphor. It is as if there is no breath. There is no whistling or grunting or straining. You sink naturally to an even flow. Because our organism is mind-body, because there is no rigid differentiation between the psychic and the physical, as the breath goes, so goes the mind. Left alone, it settles into a kind of quietness.

This quietness must be carefully understood. A quiet mind, in the sense of Lao-tzu's pool, is the deep pool that reflects everything that crosses it without distortion. In the sense of the special Zen term *wu-shin* ('no-mind') the mind is quiet when it is to itself as if it wasn't there, just as your eyes are working properly when they don't see themselves in terms of spots and blotches in front of the eye. It is not a negative quietness, an exclusive quietness that rejects the ordinary things we think about in our daily business. Those things can come and go, and the quiet mind is perfectly happy. As the sun, moon and stars can orbit in the tremendous silence of space without creating any turmoil, so the mind, when it is no-mind — when it is quiet —

becomes like space, which includes everything. This psychic process is developed hand in hand with the so-called physical process of breathing. Just as we see by a reference to the first principle, *wu-wei* — the true way of breathing — is the way of no special way.

Now we turn to another aspect of Taoist yoga that is more difficult to understand, the use of the sexual function as a means of realization. The ordinary way this sexual yogic practice is described contains the same error as the common description of the breath practice. Just as it is said that the object of the breathing practice is to hold the breath for an insufferably long time until it stops, so it is said that sexual yoga serves to prolong the sexual act indefinitely so that there is never any orgasm. The psychic force aroused thereby shifts up the spine into the *sahasraha-chakra* (in the brain) where it is transmuted into spiritual power. Yet if we go back to the first principle, we can see that beyond the misconception there is a more profound idea; but in order to comprehend it, we have to adjust some of our ideas about the nature of the sexual function.

SACREDNESS OF MARRIAGE

Most human beings seem to assume that sexual relationships are, above all, an activity. We talk of the sexual 'act'. It doesn't seem to have occurred to us that it could also be considered a form of conversation, not as an action. We regard sex as an action because we have anxiety about it. After all, for many centuries sex has been regarded as a necessary but delightful evil, which we somehow may miss out on and therefore have to pursue. It is one of those things we must get and enjoy at all costs. (This is, of course, a predominately male attitude.)

Now, an attitude toward the relationship between sexual partners that is governed by this 'go out and get' mentality will always fail to attain its objective. It is the same thing as when you eat your dinner in a great hurry – you don't taste it. We aren't cats or dogs, which just wolf down their food. We humans don't have the same digestive systems – we have a long intestine inside us, not a short one – and we know very well that if we don't eat our food slowly, we don't enjoy it.

Furthermore, when we get the steak in our mouths, if we screw up our tongue and tighten our jaws to be sure that we get the last little iota of flavour, we end up with stiff muscles and a numb tongue. In other words, one does not 'get it' by trying to hold on to it. It is the same in the most fundamental biological relationship between men and women. This anxiety to prove something, to get some special result, leads to blockages, to a lack of full realization of the process.

If we follow the clues, these various sexual yoga practices seem to envisage a relationship of man and woman – and usually, I should point out, within the context of marriage, for Tantric or Taoist yoga is not promiscuous

whoopee under the name of religion. The Christian tradition had an inkling of the sacredness of marriage. It made holy matrimony a sacrament; the Church got as far as sanctifying the ritual of putting on the wedding ring and entering into holy wedlock, but never understood biological consummation to be an act of contemplation. The sexual (Tantric) style of Taoist yoga was envisaged for husband and wife or, in some cases, a spiritual wife. First, the man and woman come together without any attempt to force a particular issue. They sit and look at one another; they observe without any sense of hurry. Then as the more strictly sexual process began, the relationship unfolds in the same spirit of contemplation.

That is the meaning of the Tantric Tibetan statues that show a male and a female buddha having intercourse in the lotus posture. In that posture one does not move, one stays still. As the sexual process is allowed to develop, instead of feeling dominated or controlling, one feels carried into a life that is not one's own but is rather between both partners. One comes to experience this principle of *wu-wei*, action in accordance with the Tao, and there is a psychic unification with the partner, which is as vivid as anything could possibly be. This doesn't necessarily mean that the completion of the sexual process is stopped. It means that it is allowed to happen in its own time, not your time. The renunciation inherent in this yoga is the renunciation of domination over the act.

This means that it has the quality of a far greater exaltation – the kind of exaltation that comes to us 'unthought'.

The whole process is parallel to every teaching about the quest for God, for mystical experience or for *satori*. He who seeks shall not find because he pushes it away, so the attitude of not seeking must be fundamental. Yet remember the apparently tricky paradox: when you try to renounce seeking, you are still seeking. It always comes back to this paradox. If you engage in activity – walking, standing, sitting, lying, breathing, eating or loving – with a preconceived notion of what you think ought to happen, then you are not open to love; you are not open to surprise. A wise old fellow I once knew said that gnosis (wisdom or spiritual truth) means to be surprised at everything. When we know what we are going to get, we are seldom surprised.

SEARCHING FOR SATORI

We may in the past have had marvellous spiritual experiences – almost everyone in this world is lucky enough to experience *satori* once in their life. Perhaps it occurred when you were an adolescent; or perhaps you were having an operation and received the right kind of gas. Maybe you took LSD. Ever afterwards, you search for that experience again: 'I want it that way.' You once had a wonderful girlfriend, and now you want another just like her. That way of thinking blocks the possibility of a meeting with life. This is why meditation for Zen practitioners and Taoists means affirming that your everyday mind is the way – not the mind you ought to have or the mind you might have if you practised acceptance or concentration. We want you to look at it just the way it is right now – that's Buddha. Just like that.

Of course, many will say this is nonsense. 'The way I am now is degraded, ordinary, unevolved, not spiritual, decadent.' Yet remember this phrase from the Zenrin poem: 'At midnight, the sun brightly shines.' All right, it is midnight now. This, at this moment, is the awful dark thing we think we are. Yet the poem also says, 'This is Buddha.'

A monk once asked a Zen master, 'What is Zen?' The master replied, 'I don't feel like answering now. Wait until there is nobody else around and I'll tell you.' Some time later the monk returned to the master and said, 'There is nobody around now, Master. Please tell me about Zen.' The master took him into the garden and said, 'What a long bamboo this is! What a short bamboo that is!'

So you may be a long bamboo, you may be a short bamboo. You may be a giraffe with a long neck or a giraffe with a short neck. What you are now is the very point. There is no goal because all goals are in the future. There is only the question of what is. Look and see; see how, of its own accord, it comes to your eye.

Alan Watts, No Label

There is no Buddha, no spiritual path to follow,
no training and no realization. What are you feverishly running after?

1

THE WORKS OF ZEN

A ZEN MASTER was once asked, 'What is the most precious thing in the world?' He promptly answered, 'The head of a dead cat.'

'Why?'

'Because no one can put a price on it.'

So, we'll begin with this 'dead cat head' point of view, because this is a parable about Zen being perfectly useless. Ordinary religious philosophy seems to be highly motivated. We follow our religious doctrines because we think that they will improve us, or the world, or that they will get us somewhere. But when Bodhidharma, the legendary founder of Zen, came from India to China, he had an interview with the emperor, a pious person given to good Buddhist works. The emperor told Bodhidharma that they had built many monasteries and have had monks and nuns converted in order for scriptures to be translated. 'Is there no merit in this?' he asked.

'No merit whatever,' Bodhidharma replied.

The emperor imagined that the whole purpose of Buddhism was to do good work, so that one gained merit and received a better incarnation in the next life. Astounded, the emperor asked, 'What, then, is the first principle of the holy doctrine?'

Bodhidharma replied, 'It is empty, and there is nothing holy.'

'Who are you to stand before us?' the emperor

When you gaze at something but see — nothing; when you listen for a sound but cannot hear it; when you try to grasp it and find it has no substance — then these things that go beyond your mind are moulded together in the One.

demanded. 'If you are not a holy man, by what merit do you gain access to the royal presence?'

'I don't know,' Bodhidharma said.

So Bodhidharma told the emperor that there was nothing to be gained, no benefit whatever, and this is the most peculiarly difficult thing to understand. Zen is a point of view — philosophical, religious, metaphysical or whatever you want to call it — that values uselessness at its purest.

THE WHICH FOR WHICH THERE IS NO WHICHER

If we think about it, we find that in the Roman Catholic view God is also a perfectly useless being. When we think of usefulness we think of material things or of events or processes serving some end. But Saint Thomas Aquinas compared the wisdom of God to a game, to play, because he said that games were played for play's sake and not for any future goal that might be obtained from them. Therefore, games reflect divine wisdom, and, as every Christian knows, the final triumph is the contemplation of the beatific vision: to behold God directly.

Just imagine somebody who arrives in heaven to be confronted by the beatific vision and who says: 'So what? What is the use of it?' According to Christianity, this vision of God is the end to which all purposes lead, the moment in which all purposes are fulfilled. It is the which for which there is no whicher. Therefore, it is quite useless in itself because it does not lead to anything beyond it – it is the end. In the same way, what we are concerned with in Zen is an end. So we cannot expect to get any form of ethics or a system of philosophy from Zen. It has no derivatives, because it is a which for which there is no whicher.

In this sense, one might apply to Zen a phrase that Saint Paul once used to describe the Crucifixion: 'To the Jews, a stumbling block; to the Greeks, foolishness' (the Jews representing the ethical people, the moralists, and the Greeks representing the philosophers). From the standpoint of both the moralists and the philosophers, Zen is a stumbling block and foolish. To summarize what Zen is we could

Give up trying to be so learned and things will become easier. Is there any difference between a 'yes' and a 'no' said insincerely? Is there a difference between being angry and pretending not to be?

say quite simply that it is the recognition that, as you are at this moment – without any additions, any monkey business whatsoever – you are a buddha. Or, in other words, you are perfect. You have nothing further to do – you have arrived. There is no place to go, no goal to achieve in life other than what there is at this very moment.

Life's immense richness and marvels, just as they are now, are normally overlooked because we always think there is something else ahead. We could say (in a clumsy way) that everything, exactly the way it is now, is perfectly right, and this is not meant in a Pollyanna-ish sense, when we want to believe that everything, no matter how evil, is playing a part in some great cosmic drama that is going to work out in the end. Not at all. The way life is in actuality is the end; the

screaming of a person tormented with cancer, at this very moment, is 'right' in a manner so positive as to render feeble the ordinary meaning of the word 'right'.

EVERYTHING IS EVERYTHING

Yet in saying that, we have said something outrageous, and, from the standpoint of the philosophical Greeks, the statement doesn't mean anything. It is pure nonsense, because to say 'Everything is right' cancels out the meaning of the 'right'. After all, as any logician knows, right is meaningful only in contrast with wrong. If everything is right and nothing is wrong, from a logical standpoint one is saying no more than 'Everything is everything'. This is exactly what we admit in Buddhist philosophy, not as a logical principle or a proposition but as an exclamation!

What we have said is not the final clause in a process of reasoning but an attempt to express an experience, an experience of such strength that when we attempt to utter it in words it obliterates language; so we are compelled to utter nonsense. To say that

ABOVE Life's immense richness and marvels, just as they are now, are normally overlooked because we always think there is something else ahead.

everything just as it is at this very moment is right, or very nearly so, is the Tao, God or Buddha. But just as we are about to say these words, they don't make sense any more. There is a beautiful Chinese poem that says:

Taking chrysanthemums along the
    eastern fence,
Gazing in silence at the southern hills,
The birds flit homeward
Through the soft mountain air of dusk.
In all these things there is a deep meaning,
But just as we were about to express it
We suddenly forgot the words.

This 'non-sense' articulates that everything at this moment is perfectly right, there are no other conclusions to be derived. It does not lead to any system of philosophy, and you cannot rest anything on it, because it is not a first word but a last word. It is meaningless in the way that 'God' in the Christian tradition is meaningless. Since He is not a symbol, He does not point to anything beyond Himself. 'Meaning', strictly speaking, is a property of symbols, of words that signify something other than themselves.

THE DANGER OF ZEN
Applying the same principle – this experience of fundamental, catastrophic rightness – is not a premise for making any inferences about conduct. It cannot be used to bolster the brotherhood of man. We cannot say that because we are all one we should treat each

The Tao takes from those who have too much, and gives it to those who have too little or nothing. What kind of person is it who has more than he needs? And gives it out, and gives it freely? Only a being that is filled with the Tao.

other as brothers. For if we are all one – if all things are one – it is equally 'one' to murder one's grandmother to collect her legacy. Evidently, you cannot derive all conduct from Zen. A Zen proverb says: 'If you are a real man, you can freely drive off the farmer's ox or snatch food from the mouth of a starving man.' In short, anything goes. It is perfectly obvious, when we talk of Zen, that there is the inherent potential for immense danger.

That is why I cannot stress enough the assumption behind the study of Zen that its students should be intellectually mature and disciplined in the ways of their culture. Zen is not for children. It is for people who are highly trained in the particular disciplines of their culture, whatever they may be. For the

Chinese, this meant the Confucian way of life, which Zen introduced into Japan. For us, it might mean the discipline of one's religion, one's profession or one's art or of ordinary manners and morals. Zen comes after discipline. It is not to be thought of as we in the West tend to think of religion. We look to our religions to bolster our social institutions, and we expect our religions to teach moral conduct to our children. These are very important and indispensable functions of

religion. Zen is not the same kind of thing – it is a path to liberation. So please do not think of Zen as some wonderful new religion to take the place of other religions or other disciplines. Zen is beyond that. It does not displace something we already have in our culture; it adds to it.

But, one might ask, what does it add? Nothing – except the wonder of the perfectly useless. So we can appreciate what Zen involves only by virtue of a peculiar attitude. We must be able to approach it without seeking anything, without any intention. Being 'without intention' is the fundamental meaning of the

important Taoist and Zen term *wu-wei*, which has a complex meaning. *Wu-wei* means 'no doing or striving or purpose'. So it can mean naturalness: what is uncontrived, what happens without being sought. The most marvellous things that ever happen to us in life are all fundamentally uncalculated. Imagine the great discovery of an inventor, who, in the process of looking for something else altogether, happens to run across the more significant discovery while walking to the bar to get a drink (to make himself happier), quite unexpectedly meeting a friend (who makes him even happier). So when we have the fundamental attitude of not seeking, we are open to experience the fullness of what is going on now.

KNOWING WHO WE ARE

The roughness and directness of the Zen manner serve to jolt us into waking up and seeing where we are. If you want to know what reality is, there is only one way to find out – that is, to look and say: 'I'm not going to believe what I have been told. I'm not going to take anything at second-hand.' We have to see for ourselves. Where are you? Where is yesterday? Where is tomorrow? Where is the history by which most of us identify ourselves? When we are asked who we are, we

Do things wu-wei, by doing nothing. Achieve without trying to achieve anything – savour the taste of what you cannot taste.

never respond directly; instead, we always say who we were.

To establish the legal, official reality of your existence, you produce a birth certificate, and that is the historical record of your birth. It doesn't say anything about who you are and therefore amounts to a kind of fiction. Yet notice that from a legal standpoint, unless you can prove that you were, you aren't. And this is really very profound, because it shows that our so-called ego, our self-existence, is purely a phenomenon of the past. It has no reality in the present. If we carefully observe the nature of our present reality, we discover therein no ego. If we look carefully, we find that we don't exist.

When Eka (in Chinese, Hui-k'o), the second patriarch of Zen, came to Bodhidharma he said, 'Master, I have no peace

RIGHT *Wu-wei... can mean naturalness: what is uncontrived... the most marvellous things that ever happen to us in life are all fundamentally uncalculated.*

Five colours blind the eye.

Five notes deafen the ear.

Five tastes deaden the mouth.

Wanting what's precious,

you do what distorts your being.

The Wise One knows this in his

gut, and is guided by instinct.

of mind. Please pacify my mind.' The original Chinese word, *shin*, which we translate in English as 'mind', doesn't mean 'mind' quite in the cortical sense. *Shin* also means heart, and when the Chinese speak of the shin they point not to the heart but to the middle of the upper body. So the *shin* is the centre of one's psychic life in both the conscious and the unconscious aspects. It is right where you feel your own existence. Eka actually said: 'I have no peace of *shin*.' In other words, the centre of his life, his very self, was not at peace.

Being a practical man, Bodhidharma told Eka, 'Well, bring out your *shin* here, and I'll pacify it.'

But the practitioner replied, 'When I look for it, I can't find it.'

Bodhidharma told him, 'There, it is pacified.'

Thus Eka was awakened, because he came to himself and was sensible; when he looked for this precious self, it wasn't there. In other words, he was deluded in much the same way as if I were to put out all the lights, light an incense stick and whirl it around in my hand. You would see a circle of fire because your retina would preserve the trace of the moving point as a retinal memory. But if you observed carefully you would know there was no circle, simply the point of fire. The great Zen master Dogen, who lived around 1200 CE and helped introduce Zen into Japan, put it this way:

One should not say that the firewood becomes the ashes. There is firewood at its place, and then later there are ashes at their place. There is first firewood, and then there are ashes. But the firewood does not become the ashes.

The same thought is expressed by T.S. Eliot in the Four Quartets when he says (to paraphrase him playfully) that 'those passengers who have boarded the train and are settled down reading their newspapers are not the same passengers who left the platform, nor will they be those who will arrive at their destination'.

In order to understand that point of view we must not be intellectually analytical; instead, we must have a certain kind of rather simple, direct stupidity. This is a very helpful

ABOVE You would see a circle of fire... but if you observed carefully you would know there was no circle, simply the point of fire.

state of mind. It is like the person who can always avoid psychology – the simple fellow who, when presented with the Rorschach ink blot test and asked to describe what he sees, says: 'I see an ink blot.' You are not going to catch him out with this kind of approach! We can observe and see that the only reality in which we live is the now, and in this way Zen is not stupidity as much as simplicity of approach.

Let me make this clear. Suppose that tomorrow something dreadful is going to happen to us – perhaps we are going to have an operation or we are going to be arrested by the police and sent to prison. Now, what can that do to us at this moment? It can, of course, create all sorts of curious sensations in the pits of our stomachs, cause the palms of our hands to sweat and send creepy-crawlies up our spine, but it can do no more than that. That is the limit of what any future catastrophe can do to us now. If we realize that we are, at this moment, beyond the reach

of that catastrophe, save for those creepy-crawlies, and that when disaster actually happens to us we will have time enough then to deal with it is a marvellous revelation.

The problem, however, is that the moment we begin to try to live in the eternal now something goes wrong. Instead, we find the difficulty that stands in our way is that we are being purposive about it. We are trying on purpose to be without purpose. We are making living in the present a goal to be attained. It's the same predicament a person finds himself in on being told he is affected: he tries to be natural and so puts on an act of being natural. So this is the problem to which Zen addresses itself: it shows one how to get out of that vicious circle, and it applies to every sphere of human activity.

DEMONSTRABLY ZEN

We say that to love is to be unselfish, but the moment I am unselfish on purpose the whole effect is ruined. And what are we to do about that? How is one to live in the eternal now? How is one to wake up to the reality of this moment without doing it on purpose? In Zen, of course, there are ways of communicating this attitude by direct demonstration, by enabling the student to come across it — to fall into it without intending to do so.

PREVIOUS SPREAD Those passengers who boarded the train are not the same ones who left the platform, nor will they be those who will arrive at their destination.

The best way to run the world is to let it take its course — and get yourself out of the way of it!

In our ordinary life it can seem to us that we are natural only occasionally, and only rarely do we live thoroughly in the moment. What Zen proposes is that it is to be our habitual and constant way of life. So the question arises again: how is it to be done? Of course, it is not done somehow, it is done no-how, rather like this. Suppose that as you listen to someone speaking you have some difficulty in following or paying attention. Yet you know very well that if you try to concentrate on what they are saying, you will instead be distracted by your efforts to concentrate and you won't think about what they are saying. So the more you try to attend to them, the more you will fail to do so. This is just the same as when you say to yourself: 'No, I mustn't try but simply be here and now.' This seems to put you in a dreadful predicament. It is like the proverb from eastern India that says that if you think about a monkey while taking medicine the medicine won't work, and so the trick is not to think of the monkey when you

ABOVE When you begin to concentrate on the now, you can't find it. The more you think about this instant, the more infinitesimally short the instant becomes.

are taking medicine. Now, as you read these words, one thing will be perfectly clear: whether you are attending to what I write or not, if you don't close your eyes or squint too hard you will understand the words on sight. Your mind works by itself, and you can't stop it.

In exactly the same way, when you consider the matter of living in this eternal now and you begin to concentrate on the now, you can't find it. The more you begin to think about this present instant, the more infinitesimally short the instant becomes. It may appear to you that you are living in a veritable non-existent no-man's-land between the extremely real past and the extremely real but intangible future. So you may become anxious and feel you have absolutely no time to live in, no time at all, no time for anything.

We have watches marked out with little hairlines, and if we wear them and look at them often enough we begin to get anxious that these hairlines are all there is. We are never alive, because we are alive only as the second hand crosses the hairline. As you think

Confront it — it has no head;

come behind it — it has no tail.

If people could only follow

the ancient way, they would

be masters of the moment.

If you know this way, you have

seen the timeless way of the Tao.

about it, there is no time at all. The instant is never there when we try to lay hold of it. This is what Buddhism means when it speaks about the evanescent quality of the world. In strict Buddhist philosophy the real world is neither permanent nor impermanent, but it says the world is impermanent in that it seems to us impermanent — exactly to the degree that we are trying to grasp it. When you chase your shadow, it runs away as quickly as you pursue it. So in every way, as we try to pin down time, it's gone.

We have to understand, then, that just as with hearing a voice or seeing words on the page, as the

sound comes to our ear or the sight to our eyes, so the moment stays with us. There is no question of finding this moment, of sticking with it, of going along with it — we have no alternative, and we can't do anything else. That too, in a way, is gratifying to know. In the words of E'no (in Chinese, Huineng), the sixth patriarch of Zen:

In this moment there is nothing that comes to be.
In this moment there is nothing that ceases to be.
Thus there is no birth and death to be brought
*   to an end.*
Wherefore the absolute tranquillity of nirvana is
*   this present moment.*
Though it is at this moment, there is no limit to
*   this moment. And herein is eternal delight.*

So when you attempt to be fully and completely aware of this instant and find out what is real, you will discover — naturally, in the beginning — that you are trying to know, that you are intending; you are looking at this experience purposefully to get something out of it. This is only natural. Then you will come to realize that, to the degree you are making an effort, you are preventing yourself from getting anything out of it. We look on life as somehow apart from ourselves, as something to be pursued as if it were a barrel of beer — we want to get something out of it — but our experience is actually as much ourselves as it is the other. This is what is meant by the Zen phrase 'Every puddle contains the entire moon'. If there is no moon in the sky, there is no moon in the water. If there is no water on the ground, there is no moon in the water. In the same way, if there is nothing to see, there is no sight. If there is no one to see it, there is no sight. So the experience of 'I' and 'Thou' depends equally on the existence of the subject and the object. In the words of a Zen poem:

> The trees show the bodily form of
> the wind;
> The waves show the spiritual vitality of
> the moon;
> If there were no tree waving
> We would not know that the wind had
> any power;
> And if there are no waves
> The moon cannot break itself into a thousand pieces
> and dance.

When you perceive the external world, what do you see? You see yourself. You see what is in

Wait for the right moment.

Be empty, be still.

Watch everything just come and go.

Emerging from the Source,

returning to the Source.

This is the way of nature.

the retina of your eye, what is inside your nerves. On the other hand, when you look at yourself, what do you see? Equally, you see the external world. The relationship is mutual. Because of this mutuality, there is no final, real possibility of one getting anything out of the other. You cannot treat the external world as a barrel of beer – although, happily, it sometimes includes a barrel of beer. To try to get something from the world is like chewing one's own tongue for its flavour. This vulture-like approach to the moment is quickly seen to be unworkable. If you try very hard to get something out of the moment, you will come to the conclusion that it can't be done, and although you are, indeed, still trying to get something out of the present because you can't help yourself, that's the way it is. If I find I am trying to pin this moment down, well then, I'm trying to pin it down and there is nothing to be done about it. Notice that it is here all the same. In that moment you begin to see that to live in the present you do not have to achieve an accepting frame of mind. You have to discover yourself as you are, not as you will be in the next minute. Even as you are grasping and trying to get something out of it, that's the moment – it does not begin when you have time to adjust and be different. Doesn't that make Zen sound easy? Nothing to do. Really! I mean it – nothing.

Some of you might ask how, in the name of heaven, does that reconcile with what you find

ABOVE *The waves show the spiritual vitality of the moon… If there are no waves The moon cannot break itself into a thousand pieces and dance.*

going on in Japan. There, if you decide to study Zen seriously under a master and you enter a monastery, you encounter terrific discipline. You meditate for hours and may work for thirty years, but the teacher is always saying to you: 'Go on, get after it. Raise up a great spirit of inquiry, work with all your might to get to the bottom of what your koan ('meditation problem') means.' You will see all those monks scrupulously trying, almost snapping to attention like soldiers and doing everything at

the double. You may say to yourself: 'This is crazy. Here, we hear about Zen from people like Suzuki or Watts, who have this whimsical attitude to it, as if there is really nothing to it. Then in Japan we find these purposive, decisive, absolutely striving monks. What gives?'

Well, there are two answers. One is, of course, that sometimes the longest way round is the shortest way home. For example, if you can't relax and get to sleep, one possible remedy is to go and run six times around the block as fast as you can. Then you realize you will just have to relax. This is the style of Zen

PREVIOUS SPREAD One way of getting people to stop seeking is to make them do it as vigorously as possible, to be sure they are utterly worn out.

one sees today. The teachers understand that one way of getting people to stop seeking is to make them do it as vigorously as possible, to be sure they are utterly worn out. It's the kill-or-cure method. And sometimes it works. Sometimes it doesn't. Either way, this was not the way Zen was originally practised in the Tang dynasty, in the time of the sixth patriarch and his immediate successor. They did not sit for hours on end thinking about koans or trying to make their minds empty. I have searched to the best of my ability through the documents of the period to try and find out what exactly was going on, and I can find nothing concerning these practices of lengthy *zazen* ('sitting meditation') except some slightly derisive remarks. But this does not mean that they were just loafing around the monastery saying that Zen was anything cute that you would happen to think of doing.

They were addressing themselves to a very fierce problem, perhaps the most profound problem in the world, which I have tried to express in the context of real self-knowledge and self-awareness. After all, there is, perhaps, a more direct way to silence, to doing-nothing and not-seeking, than wearing yourself out. To wear yourself out is a way that works for the dumb fellow who has to learn in the school of hard knocks, but someone smarter can see the

Stop talking, stop thinking, and there is nothing you will not understand. Return to the Source and you will find the meaning; pursue the Light and you will lose its Source...

paradox. He can, in other words, recognize his feeling that trying to get something out of this moment is impossible. He can ask who it is that is trying to get something out of it. Or he can simply realize, by looking at the situation, that what he is trying to do – to get something from life – is impossible. That is what those early Tang masters were trying to get across with their disciplines, very simply and directly. All the literature of the period has just that one objective. Lin-chi (or Linji), the great Rinzai (as he is known), who died about 867 CE and was one of the greatest of the masters of the Tang dynasty, would invariably

RIGHT After all, there is, perhaps, a more direct way to silence, to doing-nothing and not-seeking, than wearing yourself out.

shake his disciples and say: 'Look, can't you see? You are followers of the way.'

THE WISDOM OF DOING NOTHING

In Buddhism there is no place for effort: 'Just be ordinary and do nothing special. Relieve your bowels, pass water, eat your food, put on your clothes. When you are tired go and lie down. The ignorant will deride you, but the wise will understand.' And again: 'If any man seeks the way (the Tao), that man loses the way.' If you try to practise the Tao, the Tao will not work. Entangling circumstances will pop up competitively. Again and again the teachings underline the fact that you cannot get at it by striving or seeking. A true man responds to the ordinary circumstances of life as his direct karma. If he has to walk, he walks. If he has to sit, he sits. He hasn't any desire to become a buddha. How is it so? One of the ancients says: 'If you seek the Buddha deliberately, your buddha is just *samsara*, the squirrel cage of birth and death.'

Obviously, such a doctrine – such an attempt, rather – can easily be misunderstood. It can simply encourage a fatuous loafing around for people who think it is clever. Towards the end of the Tang dynasty Zen became a colossal success in China and received imperial favour. Enormous monasteries arose, and devout Buddhists sent their children to them as a matter of course.

Heaven and Earth are enduring, the universe can live forever, because it does not live for itself. So both last, outliving themselves.

(It was the same in eighteenth-century England, where the second son of a land-owning family usually became a clergyman, whether he had a vocation or not.) Mere boys, fourteen-year-olds, went to these tremendous Zen monasteries without having any special vocation for it. The masters – what could they do? They could say, 'Go home,' but then they would lose the parents' patronage, and they were practical, after all. So they said: 'All right, we have to bring these boys up. We have to educate them.'

There is only one way to do that: make them sit still and have them watch the monk with a big stick. It keeps them out of mischief! Also, make them study; have them study Confucian classics and Buddhist scriptures and make them learn them by heart. Make them answer questions and then, finally, leave them with an insoluble problem, with utterly foolish questions, so that in the end they will find out that there is nothing to find out. Zen training as we see it today was developed exactly like

the training you find in the Jesuit noviciate or in British public schools. It's the same kind of thing. And it is a privilege to have belonged to some of these institutions, these ecclesiastical hierarchies, because then you can recognize them wherever you find them and beware.

But they do serve their place. These monasteries produce a very fine type of personality – someone with a strong character, who is humorous, balanced and often fearless. But it is still a type, a stereotype. Occasionally, right at the end of the training – pop! – out comes a free man, who sees through the whole thing and who is truly entitled to the wonderful name given to a monk, *unsui*, which means 'cloud and water', because he drifts like clouds and flows like water. He has nowhere to go, no purpose, nothing left to achieve, nothing left to get out of life because it is all here.

Now you might say, how dull – no motivation, nothing left to do. Wouldn't this be socially disastrous if we had a lot of people who had no purpose in life? Wouldn't everything just collapse and be intolerable? First of all, if there were quite a lot of people in our culture who had no purpose in life, it would be much better in general because it would offset those who have too much and we would come to a happy medium because everyone would admit that Western civilization – even where it is no longer Christian – still has a missionary spirit. Our civilization is out to prove that it is right by converting everybody else to it, and that is always the give-away. A person who is out to convert you does not really believe what he is saying. He has to convince you to agree with him to shore up his own sense of insecurity. We Westerners feel we have to be going somewhere because we cannot sit down where we are. We have, as it were, psychological ants in our pants. We can't keep still. So a degree of purposelessness in our culture, even a very superficial kind, is nothing to be seriously afraid of.

The deeper question – whether this purposelessness would obliterate all creativity – has been proved by the historical record to be nonsense. China became intensely creative in the great age of Zen, the Song dynasty (960–1279). Zen lay behind the production of the very finest achievements of Chinese art, literature, poetry and architecture. We do not, it is true, see Zen obviously manifested in good works. Zen strongly dislikes advertising good works because it has something its students call 'secret virtue', also known as 'filling a well with snow'. You put the snow in but it vanishes; it makes no difference and leaves no trace. If, by any chance, a bodhisattva

does good, he doesn't let on that he has done it. His whole orientation is against trying, by any kind of violence, to change the world. He trusts the world to change itself in an orderly fashion. It will change itself if you leave it alone; but 'leaving it alone' does not imply walking away from the world. It means leaving the world alone knowing that you really can't walk away from it – you are part of it. No one leaves anything alone.

You begin to get the same feeling about the external world that you feel about your own body. When you see clouds blowing over your head, you feel the same way you feel about rumblings in your tummy or your breath going in and out or the beating of your heart. You realize: 'I'm doing it; those clouds – I'm moving them.' You ask me how I move them. Well, I don't know. I don't know how I breathe, but I do it. And it is the same way with the clouds. Conversely, when I lift my hand, it is not I but the whole universe that lifts it up. There are two different ways of looking at one and the same thing.

From this point of view nobody is pushing the world around, and the world is not pushing anybody around either. All of it is simply happening as it is now. There is no question of inertia, lack of activity or dissolution of the creative spirit because here it is anyhow. Just here,

RIGHT You realize: 'I'm doing it: those clouds – I'm moving them.' You ask me how I move them. Well I don't know. I don't know how I breathe, but I do it.

a universe exists. Does it need to have motivation to do it? Does the sun have to be inspired by a great sense of purpose in order to shine? Here it is anyway; and presumably, it will go on. We need not suffer from the anxiety (or indeed, the presumption) of thinking that if we don't push the world, it won't function. When we try to push it – if we are observant – we find we have nowhere to put our feet in order to give it a shove. When we try to catch this moment (to use a marvellous metaphor from R.H. Blythe), 'It is as if we were about to swat a fly, and it flew up and sat on the swatter.'

Those who think the Way is easy will find it extremely difficult.
The greatest virtue is to be empty like a valley.

2

INTRODUCTION TO ZEN PRACTICE

THE FASCINATION OF ZEN

Zen has held a strange fascination for Westerners since Dr Daisetz Suzuki published his first essays on Zen Buddhism in 1927. Many intelligent Western people were becoming, or had already become, dissatisfied with the standard varieties of their own religions. This profound dissatisfaction had begun at the close of the nineteenth century. At the same time we began to learn more about Far Eastern philosophy and religions through the work of great scholars who were translating Buddhist and Hindu texts into Western languages. By 1848 the Jesuits had translated the Tao-te Ching into French, and English translations soon became available.

What was happening was rather curious; we were receiving far more sophisticated teachings from the Asian traditions than we were receiving from the Christian or Jewish traditions. The average Westerner was exposed to an extremely unsophisticated understanding of Christianity from birth and was now comparing this religious education with the highest levels of Hinduism and Buddhism. You could not go into your parish church, even in a university neighbourhood, and find 'Meister Eckhard' for sale on the entrance table. Nor would you even find the works of Saint Thomas Aquinas; you found only little, parochial

LEFT Theosophy was very romantic and conjectured that the adepts of Buddhism were… supermen, whose lodgings were hidden in the vastness of the Himalayas.

texts, and the comparison was hardly fair to the Christian tradition.

Then in 1875 a Russian woman, H.P. Blavatsky, founded the Theosophical Society, whose doctrines and literature were a fantastic hodgepodge of Western occult traditions, with a great deal of Hindu and Buddhist lore and a smattering of Tibetan and Chinese Buddhism. Theosophy was very romantic and conjectured that the adepts of Hinduism, Buddhism, Taoism and so forth were high-order initiates and that their masters were a race of supermen, whose lodgings were hidden in the vastness of the Himalayas or perhaps even in the Andes. These adepts were inaccessible because they possessed the most dangerous secrets and occult powers. Every now and then, however, the masters would send an emissary out into the world to teach humans the ancient doctrine of liberation.

Through Theosophy, then, the West acquired an extremely glamorous impression of what Eastern wisdom might be. I remember when Dr Suzuki first came to England, the media expected him to be a master in the theosophical sense or, if not quite that, at least in touch with those who were.

So the Western concept of the Zen master – even the fact that we call teachers of Zen 'masters' – carried with it this theosophical flavour, along with a certain fawning. We have the feeling that these people possess tremendous powers, and this is largely what many expect from Zen masters. Yet the interesting thing about Zen teachers is that they are very human. They would never deign to perform a miracle.

I learned about Zen masters through my first wife, because her family went to Japan when she was about fourteen years old. They lived in Kyoto, close to the great monastery of Nanzen-ji, where the master in charge was a brilliant old teacher by the name of Nanshinken. Now, the man who is appointed to be the roshi (the spiritual leader of Nanzen-ji) is always considered the top monk of the whole bunch. But you can't expect a Zen master to be like the Pope. Although they can appear very dignified when necessary, there is always something about them that is fundamentally lacking in seriousness, even though they are endowed with sincerity. They are extraordinarily interesting people, as are their students – especially in the context of Japanese culture.

JAPANESE CULTURE

Japanese culture can seem to be terribly uptight. The Japanese are a passionate people, but they have to repress that passion because they live in a crowded country. Space is the most valuable commodity in Japan, especially living space. Eighty per cent of the territory is uninhabitable – it is a rugged land of forests and mountains – and the people are therefore crowded into twenty per cent of the country,

Most people fret about themselves and their status, but you don't have to do this. What is success? What is failure? If you have prestige and favour, all you worry about is that it'll get taken away.

so they try to handle these feelings of being pressed in through exquisite politeness, orderly behaviour and a strong sense of convention.

But this makes the average Japanese man and woman nervous. When a Japanese person giggles, it's not a sign of amusement but of embarrassment. And they are tremendously hung up on the concept of social indebtedness, whether one owes a debt to the emperor or one's parents and ancestors, or whether one is in debt to friends who have played host to you. You always take gifts with you when you go to friends' houses, but then that embarrasses your hosts, because they have to

RIGHT Zen monks appear pretty stiff. When they walk out in the street, they almost look like soldiers. They don't shuffle like other Japanese. They don't giggle.

remember to bring gifts of the same value the next time they visit you. In Japan Zen is actually a release from Japanese culture. It rids people of their hang-ups in a manner that does not embarrass the rest of society.

Zen monks, then, appear as if they are pretty stiff. When they walk out in the street, they almost look like soldiers. They don't shuffle like other Japanese; they stride. They don't giggle; they have no need, because their discipline has liberated them from the social conventions. Yet they are tactful; they pretend they are pillars of society. They exemplify an ancient tradition that is found in every society: an inner group of people who don't believe in the fairy stories they've been told and who see through the games people are playing yet don't despise them for playing those games.

Of course, the main game that everybody is playing is the survival game. We live in constant dread of sickness, death or the loss of property and status. Well, so what? Suppose you die – everybody is going to die someday. It's just harder to take when you're twenty than when you're sixty. And a Zen monk understands that if you identify completely with this particular expression of the universe, you haven't been properly educated. If you were awake, you would understand that you and the whole universe are pretending: projecting yourself at the point called here and now in the form of a human organism. You would understand this very clearly, not just as

an idea, but as a vivid sensation, in the same way you know you are sitting in this room.

$$E = MC^2$$

The object of Zen, as in other ways of liberation – Taoism, Hinduism, Sufism (Islamic mysticism) and even the Eastern Orthodox church – is to bring you to a vivid, even sensuous, realization of your true identity. All vibration is a wave of what there is, the totality of what there is. All vibration is the famous E that equals MC^2, and you are that. You always will be that; you always have been that. Accept it! Time is more or less a human illusion. There never was anything but now, and there never will be anything but now, and now is eternity.

Zen is a little unlike other branches of Hinduism and Buddhism in that Zen transmits the Buddha's enlightenment outside the scriptures. It does not depend on words and letters; it points directly to your own mind-heart. Zen, therefore, attains buddha-hood directly.

Buddha-hood is the state of being awakened into the true nature of things. Yet the real nature of things cannot be described. It is the same as if I were to ask, 'What is the true position of the stars in the Big Dipper (Great Bear)?' It depends on where you are. From

PREVIOUS SPREAD The Japanese are a passionate people, but have to repress that passion because they live in a crowded country. Space is the most valuable commodity.

People are too bound up in themselves. If they weren't so self-obsessed they'd have no need to be worried. If you can put yourself aside – then you are ready to serve the whole of the world.

one point in space they would be positioned completely differently than from another. So there is no true position for those stars. You cannot describe either their true position or their real nature. However, when you look at them and don't try to figure out their true location or nature, you see them as they are. They are just as they are from every point of view.

Thus, there is no way of putting your finger on what Buddhists call reality, or *shunyata*, which means 'voidness' in the sense that all conceptions of the real world, when made absolute, are void. It does not mean that the world is literally (in our Western sense) nothing; it means that it is no-thing. A thing is a unit of thought, a 'think'. Reality isn't a think; we cannot say what it is, but we can experience it. This is the process behind Zen: it goes about it by pointing, not telling. The 'pointing' character of Zen was what excited people about Dr Suzuki's work when he first taught Westerners about Zen. Before, Zen had seemed to us to consist of an assemblage of weird anecdotes. Its practitioners, instead of explaining, had a kind of a joke or riddle system.

E'no (Huineng), who died in the year 713 CE, explained the secret of this riddle system in a sutra. He said, if anyone asks you about secular matters, answer them in metaphysical terms. But if they ask you about anything metaphysical, answer them in terms of things worldly.

So if a student says to a Zen master, 'What is the fundamental teaching of the Buddha?' the master immediately replies, 'Have you had breakfast?'

'Yes.'

'If so, go and wash your genuflection.'

Another example: a student complains, 'Since I came to you, Master, you have never

My words are easy to

understand, and be with, and

walk in, but no one can!

My words have roots,

my actions have precedents

but people don't see this,

and so they don't see me.

given me any instruction.' The master might reply: 'How can you say that I have never given you any instruction? When you brought me tea, didn't I drink it? When you brought me rice, didn't I eat it? When you saluted me, didn't I return the salutation? How can you say that I haven't instructed you?'

The student responds, 'Master, I don't understand.'

'If you want to understand,' the master says, 'See into it directly. When you begin to think about it, it is altogether missed.'

Zen monasteries have a funny thing – a chin rest. If you spend a long time meditating, it is sometimes

convenient to have a prop for your chin. So, when a student asked his teacher, 'Why did Bodhidharma come to China?' the master responded, 'Give me that chin rest.' The student passed it to his teacher, who swung around and hit him with it.

A group of monks were walking through a forest, and suddenly the master picked up a branch, handed it to one of his disciples and demanded, 'Tell me, what is it?' The master took the branch in his hand and repeated, 'Tell me, what is it?' The disciple hesitated, so the master hit him with the branch. The master then turned to another disciple. 'What is it?' he asked. The disciple said, 'Let me have it so I can tell you.' The master threw the branch to the second disciple, who caught it and hit the master.

I was once idly discussing these stories with a Zen master. He stopped me and asked, 'You know, I've often wondered: when water goes down the drain, does it go clockwise or anticlockwise?'

'Well,' I replied, 'it might do either.'

He said, 'No, this way.'

Then he asked me, 'Which came first, egg or hen?' So I started clucking.

The master told me, 'Yes, that's right.'

ZEN RIDDLES

All these Zen riddles have simpler meanings then you would ever imagine. They are so devastatingly simple that you don't see them.

What do the people want?

Money and things.

Yet I find I have nothing,

and I don't care.

I am as unambitious

as any fool.

Everybody looks for something complicated. A Chinese Zen Buddhist once visited my daughter, who was a little girl then, and myself. He asked her, 'You know, once upon a time there was a man who kept a small gosling in a bottle. It began to grow larger and larger, until he couldn't get it out of the bottle. Now he didn't want to break the bottle and he didn't want to hurt the goose, so what should he do?' Immediately, she replied, 'Just break the bottle.' He turned to me and said, 'You see, they always get it when they are under seven.'

The technical term for this kind of Zen is *sanzen*, which means studying Zen in the form of an interchange with a teacher. These days, *sanzen* in the monasteries is very formal, but these stories all come from the Tang and Song dynasties in China, when the relationship of student to teacher was more informal. The other side of Zen is *zazen*, the practice of meditation. You can actually practise *zazen* in four ways, corresponding to what Buddhists call the 'Four Dignities' of man: walking, standing, sitting and lying. Sitting is the most common form, but you should not imagine that you must sit to meditate. *Zazen* is the art of letting your mind become still. That doesn't mean that your mind becomes blank. That doesn't mean that you block out sensory input. *Zazen* simply means that you learn how to breathe properly – that's very important – and that you stop talking to yourself; the interminable chatter inside the skull comes to rest. I should add that there are several distinct schools of Zen, with different methods and different approaches. My approach to Zen is again somewhat different from other people's approaches, but Buddhism has always had this kind of elasticity.

INVITATIONS TO ZEN

You may have some difficulty in being accepted by a teacher, because Buddhists are not missionaries. They don't send out invitations saying, 'Come to our jolly church'. They wouldn't dream of doing that; it's up to you to seek them out. So it is difficult to get into a Zen school, for it isn't like a Christian monastery, where the monks take life vows of

RIGHT You can practise *zazen* in four ways, what Buddhists call the 'Four Dignities' of man: walking, standing, sitting and lying. Sitting is the most common form.

Most people seem to be bright
and sharp — and how do I feel?
Like a blunted sword.
The people, the people are like
the waves of the sea,
and I am drifting between them
wherever they are blown.

poverty, chastity and obedience. It's more like a theological seminary. The monk, or seminarian, as he might more accurately be called, stays there for a number of years until he feels he has got what he went for. The teacher, the master, is usually unmarried, but that does not prevent him from having girlfriends. They are not as stringent about sex in Zen as they are in other forms of Buddhism. The whole atmosphere in a monastery is fascinating. Everybody is alive — they are all working, but they are very open.

Early in the morning, and at certain times of the day, Zen monks meet and sit cross-legged on their mats for meditation. In one sect they meditate on a koan, which means a 'case', in the sense of a legal case establishing a precedent. One example of a koan is: when the great master Joshu (who lived in the Tang dynasty) was asked, 'Does a dog have buddha-nature?' he replied '*Mu*', which means 'no'. Everybody knows that dogs have buddha-nature. So why did the great master say '*Mu*'?

Hakuin, the haiku poet, invented a koan. Borrowing from the Chinese proverb 'One hand cannot make a clap', he asked: 'What is the sound of one hand clapping?' Of course, it's phrased differently in Japanese than English — it sounds like a very complicated problem. The student meditates on the problem and begins by trying to arrive at an intellectual answer. If he takes that answer back to the teacher during *sanzen*, the teacher simply rejects it automatically, time after time. People get desperate about their koans. They go to all sorts of lengths to try and answer them because they don't realize how simple the answers are: that's what people always overlook. If you would answer Hakuin's koan in English, it gives it to you as it is stated: 'what' is the sound of one hand clapping. But it's very difficult for people to become that simple. You can become simple only through meditation, when you stop all the words and see things directly.

Accomplished Zen people are very, very direct. Their life is completely simplified because they know there is only this present moment: no past; no future. By not being direct, we create a great deal of trouble with

other people. However, Zen is more concerned with man's relation to nature than it is with interpersonal relations. Where are your views of life and death? There is an inscription that hangs in Zen monasteries that says: 'Birth and death is a serious event. Time waits for no one.' Zen begins with a clarification of our relationship with existence.

And therefore it lies at a more primary level than the contemporary encounter group, which is primarily concerned with personal relationships. I don't think you can set up harmonious personal relationships until you're at one with yourself and you're at one with the sky, the trees and the rocks, and the water and the fire. Then you are fundamental – you are really alive.

From that position you can relate much better to other people because you don't come

PREVIOUS SPREAD

I don't think you can set up
harmonious relationships 'til
you're at one with yourself
and… with the sky, the trees
and the rocks, and the water.

at them with a 'poor little me who doesn't really belong' attitude. Most of us are terribly apologetic about our own existence, as if we were here on probation. Some people, though, overcompensate for this inferior status in the universe with boastfulness and aggression towards others.

DOGEN

When Dogen – who lived around 1200 CE, studied Zen and founded a great monastery – came back from China, his countrymen asked him, 'What did you learn in China?'

He said: 'I learned that their eyes are horizontal and their noses are perpendicular.' Now, in all these things, don't search for a deep symbolism. They are not symbolic, they are absolutely direct. When somebody says that the fundamental principle of Buddhism is 'a cypress tree in the garden', you are not to understand that this is some sort of pantheistic doctrine in which the cypress tree is a manifestation of the godhead.

The point is that Zen practice uses words with directness to get beyond words. All of us hypnotize people with words. Children, for instance, have no antibodies against words, so they get absolutely frantic when someone calls them a sissy. They become desperate about name-calling because we give words power over us. These are spells, you see, and all magicians ensnare people with spells and incantations because they use words to beguile.

From infancy we are told who we are, what our identity is, what our expectations should be, what we ought to get out of life and what class we belong to – and we believe the whole thing. We come to sense this spell as we sense the hard wood of a table, and we think it is real, whereas it is a bunch of hogwash. It is an amusing game if you know that's all it is; then it can be played with elegance. The more you know that this game is only an illusion, the better you can play.

NO PURPOSE

Zen practice is not like any other form of exercise; it is not done for a purpose. You may ask, 'How can I possibly do something that is not being done for a purpose?' because you have a fixed idea (which is part of the hypnosis) that everything you do should have a purpose. I once saw Soke An Sasaki, a great Zen master, sitting in his gorgeous golden robe and burning incense, with a scripture open in front of him. Commenting on a passage in the sutra, he said: 'Fundamental principle of Buddhism is purposelessness. Most important is to attain state of no purpose. When you drop fart, you don't say nine o'clock I drop fart. It just happens.' In Chinese their word for nature is *tzu-jan* (in Japanese, *shizen*), which means 'what is so of itself' or what we would

When the wild geese fly over the lake, The water does not intend to reflect them And the geese have no mind To cast their image.

call 'spontaneity'. A tree has no intention to grow. Water has no intention to flow. Clouds have no intention to blow.

When the wild geese fly
over the lake
The water does not intend to reflect them
And the geese have no mind
To cast their image.

Now, this worries us. First of all, we think that spontaneity is mere capricious action. Yet there is nothing capricious about the way a tree grows. It is a highly intelligent design. So is a bird. So are you. Many people who don't understand Zen think that spontaneity means just doing anything, and the more it looks like anything, the more spontaneous it is. They have a preconception of spontaneity: that a person behaving spontaneously would probably be messy, vulgar, impolite or rude.

Spontaneity is the way your hair grows. It's not the way you think your hair ought to grow – it's the way it happens. It is really a high order of intelligence. In the discipline of Zen, we are trying to move into the place where we can use that intelligence in everyday life. Yet you see you can't get it on purpose. Purpose, motivation always spoils it. You might ask, 'How do I get rid of purpose?' On purpose? To

ask that question is to show how tied up you are in the thinking process. Yet you cannot force that process to stop. You have to see it as nonsense, interminable babble in your mind.

BABBLING THOUGHTS

So you learn to listen to your thoughts, to let the mind think anything it wants to think, yet not to take it seriously. Even the idea of your doing this is babble in the head. Eventually this comes about, but without bothering about any 'eventually', because in this state there is no future. Purpose is always wrapped up in thoughts of the future. What bothers Western people about purposelessness is that it suggests that life has no meaning, no purpose. 'Well,' I would ask, 'What's so bad about that? What sort of meaning would you like it to have?'

When people try to define the meaning of life, they say: 'I think that we are all part of a plan and that we are all working towards the great fulfilment that will come one day — perhaps after we're dead, perhaps in a future life. And then, there will be a great *gazuzi* [prize]. There will be a galluptious, glorious goody at the end of the line. That's what we are all in this for, to be part of that; and it will all be very, very important because it won't just be something trivial, it will be something extremely holy.'

'Well,' I ask, 'What is

LEFT Spontaneity is the way your hair grows. It's not the way you think your hair ought to grow — it's the way it happens. It is really a high order of intelligence.

The Tao of Heaven doesn't struggle, but it wins through. It doesn't ask, yet it always hears the answer. It has no desires, yet everything works out as planned. And though the net of Heaven is wide, not even the tiniest whisper escapes it.

your idea of "very holy"?' Nobody really knows the answer to that. They think about church and the way the medieval artists used to represent heaven, with everybody sitting in choir stalls. I must say, hell looks much more fun. There, at least, there is some kind of sado-masochistic orgy taking place, but heaven must be insufferably dull. So this holy event at the end of time makes for a very, very depressing future, I can assure you. The point is this: when you follow these ideas through, when you inquire what this goody might be, what progress truly is, you realize that you just don't know. It is at that point that one asks the meditator: 'But aren't you there already?'

Its surface doesn't shine, but nor is its base dull.
Given this, it is only knowable as no-thing.

3

THUSNESS

THE SANSKRIT WORD *tathata* is a very strange word, often translated into English as 'thusness' or 'suchness'. *Tathata* is built on the Sanskrit root *tat*, which is etymologically the root of our word 'that'. In India parents assume that this is the first word a baby says. We all know that babies say 'da-da-da'. In our highly patriarchal culture, we assume that the baby is addressing its father, so 'da-da' means 'father'. But in India, where the ancient cultures were matriarchal, it didn't mean 'mother'. It meant 'da', the fundamental word of all words: the baby pointing to something and saying 'that'.

When the baby wakes up, he or she is an aperture through which it looks at everything and exclaims 'da'. So *tathata* means 'da-da-da'. In the same way, the founding artists of the Dada movement in the West called it Dada so they could go beyond words and names. So *tathata* is a fundamental word, and we have great difficulty translating it because, in a way, it is a meaningless word.

In order to discuss this subject properly, I have to give you an introduction to Buddhism, because this is all part of Buddhist philosophy, and the original context of Buddhism is Indian philosophy. The first thing to understand about Buddhism is that it does not have a doctrine in the sense that Christianity has

LEFT Buddhism, then, is a method and the method involves dialogue: a discussion, an interchange, between a teacher and a student.

The one who really knows, knows without books. The so-called learned know nothing. The Wise One holds nothing of himself back. He uses all he has for you, and that is his reward. He gives all he is and that is why he is rich.

a doctrine. There could be no such thing as a Buddhist creed. Buddhism is traditionally called the *buddha-dharma*, and *dharma* is a Sanskrit word that means 'method'. Buddhism, then, is a method, and the method involves dialogue: a discussion, an interchange, between a teacher and a student, between the Buddha and his disciples.

To understand the point of this interchange, we need to know that the word buddha comes from the Sanskrit root *budh*, which means 'to be awake'. So a buddha is a person who is awake; it is therefore a title, not a proper name or the name of a divinity. There are many gods (angels, we might call them) in Buddhism. Yet they are considered inferior to a buddha — the gods are not yet fully awakened.

Be a channel for the energies here. Weave them in a true and practical way so they can link up with the Way and become one again. Oneness generates everything. The Wise One never tries to break up the whole.

THE BUDDHIST WORLD

Buddhism divides the world into six areas, and this division is very important to any understanding of Buddhism. These six divisions are not literal; they may equally refer to states of human consciousness. We begin by drawing a circle, the wheel of life. In the top section of the circle we have the *deva* world. *Deva* is like our word 'devil', but it actually means 'angels'. And the reason is this: hundreds of years ago, when the Persians battled the Aryans (the ancient northern Indians), who called their gods *devas*, the Persians insulted them by using that word to mean 'devils'. The *asura* (spirits of wrath) were opposite Ahura (who in Persia is the Lord of Light). So we have the *devas* on top of the circle, and next to them on one side are the *asuras*, the powers of divine wrath (in the sense of energy, vigour). Below on the circle, opposite the *devas* are the *narakas*, the purgatories where everybody is as unhappy as they can be. Then there are animals in another section, and men and women in yet another. Here are things called *pretors*, who are frustrated spirits with very large stomachs and very small mouths. The result, therefore, is the rat race of existence, called *samsara* in Sanskrit, which describes the wheel of birth and death.

The zenith is as high as you can get, and the bottom of the circle, the nadir, is as low as you can get. Up, of course, also implies down. So while you are trying to get better and better, when you get to the best, you can only move on to the worst. So you go 'round and round', ever chasing the illusion that there is something outside yourself, outside your here and now.

A buddha is somebody who has woken up and discovered that the rat race of existence – the cycle of births and deaths – leads nowhere. Buddhism says that there is only one point on the wheel of existence from which you can become a buddha, and that is here on earth, as a human. Buddha-nature is inaccessible to all other realms of existence, to the realms of the gods, the spirits and the animals. The *devas* are

LEFT Buddhism says that there is only one point on the wheel of existence from which you can become a buddha, and that is here on earth, as a human.

PREVIOUS SPREAD Only in the middle position of man – the position of potential equanimity – can you free yourself from the wheel… and become a buddha.

too happy to worry about becoming buddhas, the *narakas* are too miserable, the *asuras* too angry, the animals too dumb, and the *pretors* too frustrated. Only in the middle position of man – the position of potential equanimity – can you free yourself from the wheel of existence and become a buddha.

So the Buddha is the axle point, the 'still point of the turning world' to use T.S. Eliot's phrase. The Buddha is also the navel, which is why yogis are said to contemplate their navels. The navel in this sense isn't the tummy, it is the navel of the world. A buddha, then, is one who awakens from the illusion of *samsara*, from the thought that there is something to get out of life, that tomorrow will bring it to you, that in the course of time it will be all right. A buddha is free from the compulsion to chase time – from the ridiculous desire to quench thirst by drinking salt water.

THE SOCIAL SYSTEM OF BUDDHISM

We can exemplify this more clearly by relating Buddhism to the social system in which it arose. A Buddhist monk is sometimes called a *shramana*, a word closely allied to the English word 'shaman'. A shaman is the holy man in a hunter-gatherer culture – it isn't settled, it

A man on tiptoe cannot walk with ease. The man who strides ahead is bound to tire. The one who insists on his view of life can never learn from others. People like these, say the Wise Ones, are as useless as the left-over food at a feast.

isn't agrarian. There is a strong, important difference between a shaman and a priest. A priest has received his ordination from his superiors. He receives something from a handed-down tradition. A shaman, however, receives his enlightenment by going off into the forest to be completely alone. A shaman is a man, in other words, who has undergone a solitary transformation. He has gone into seclusion to find out who he really is, because it is very difficult to discover that around other people.

Other people are constantly telling you who you are, but their views have been shaped by laws that have been devised by the culture, by the behaviour patterns earlier generations created and by the things told to us. Even the

ABOVE You go deep into
the forest, stop talking
and even stop thinking
words; you let yourself be
absolutely alone, and you
listen to the great silences.

fact that we are all called
particular names and, not
least of all, the fact that
we live among people in a
state of ceaseless chatter,
add to our confusion. If
you want to find out who
you were before your father and mother
conceived you – who you really are – you will
probably have to go off by yourself. You go
deep into the forest, stop talking and even stop
thinking words; you let yourself be absolutely
alone, and you listen to the great silences.
And then, if you are lucky, you recover from
the illusion that you are just 'little me, this
so-and-so', and you attain the state of nirvana,
which means the 'blown-out state', the
relieved state, the sigh of relief.

Nirvana may be translated into English as

'Whew!' At last you have discovered that you
don't have to survive. You can survive, of
course, but you discover that what you really
are doesn't have to survive; it is what it is.
The real you is it, or that *tat tvam asi*, 'that
thou art', as the Hindus say.

In the normal life of India, which is not a
hunting culture but a settled culture, there are
priests. But there is also a role beyond the
priest. When men or women have fulfilled their
lives in the world, they are free to quit their
status in society and become what are called
'forest dwellers'. This may go back to India's
ancient hunting cultures. By the time the
historical Buddha was born (about 600 BCE),
the Hindu system had become somewhat
decadent. It isn't altogether clear to present-
day scholars what had happened to it, but we
are certain that it was in need of reform. As a

The Wise do not collect for themselves. The more they give to others, the more they possess of their own. The Way of Heaven is to benefit others and not to harm. The way of the Wise is to act — but not compete.

young man, the Buddha, troubled by the great problems that disturb us all – the problem of suffering and the problem of not knowing what this universe is about – endeavoured to follow the methods currently being used by holy men to answer these questions. At that time the main spiritual practice was an ascetic discipline: starvation, arduous meditation practices, self-flagellation and things of that nature. According to legend, he practised these austerities for seven years, only to discover that they did not lead him to liberation. Other practitioners knew they hadn't worked for themselves either, but they felt that they just weren't practising hard enough.

The Buddha, however, discovered another path, which he called the 'middle way' – the middle way between austerity and indulgence; a way that led to liberation from the rat race of *samsara*, neither through austerity nor through seeking pleasure.

Even today, austerity and pleasure-seeking are the two common paths. Some say the whole point of life is to enjoy it, to get the most out of it. Others, who have burned their fingers in the pursuit of pleasure, say instead, 'Let us torment ourselves.' And a lot of people enjoy this. I went to Mexico this summer [1967] to study the uniquely Mexican expression of Catholicism, where they make a great cult of suffering. I was puzzled about this and wanted to understand it. Everywhere I went, I saw these ghastly, tormented Christs, dripping with blood and hanging in contorted poses on crosses. I realized that there are certain people who find sitting on the tip of a spike to be the most real place in the world; when you are on the tip of a spike, you know you are there – there is no doubt about it. You also know that by sitting on the spike you are paying for all your guilt: as long as you hurt, you are all right. Those ancient *shramanas* were doing something quite similar.

However, the Buddha became enlightened (became a buddha) the moment he saw the futility of trying to force his way to freedom. He recognized that he had been trying

RIGHT Even today, austerity and pleasure-seeking are the two common paths. Some say the whole point of life is to enjoy it, to get the most out of it.

to take the kingdom of heaven by storm.

The Buddha also found that the true path, the middle way, required dialogue. Instead of telling his followers to go off on their own and practise terrific austerities, he engaged them in a dialectic, in conversations that revealed to them that they were already the buddha-nature they were trying to become. For in Buddhism solitude is only a preliminary gesture, a transitional phase on the way to becoming a *bodhisattva*.

A *bodhisattva* is somebody who has given up the world in some way, has taken on the robe and has found what he was seeking; but his finding it is simultaneous with his return into society. A *bodhisattva* is distinct from a *pratyeka-buddha*, one who leaves society and never returns. Buddhists consider the *bodhisattva* to have a superior attainment and superior insight. A *bodhisattva* returns to encourage others to find their own buddha-nature, for such a person has realized that we all suffer because we try to cling to an ever-changing world and because we imagine we are a separate self. He returns to help us realize for ourselves that everything exists only in relation to everything else: there are no separate things, no real selves, no souls or egos.

So at the heart of the *buddhadharma* ('Buddhist method') is relationship and dialogue, the beginning of which is not necessarily the same thing as the end. The reason for this is that the experience of

Learn to yield and be soft, if you want to survive. Learn to bow and you will stand in your full height. Learn to empty yourself and be filled by the Tao… the way a valley empties into a river.

awakening (which constitutes the foundation of Buddhism) can't be stated or at least, if it can be stated, it can't be articulated so that the mere statement will communicate the experience to somebody else. The experience itself is the culmination of an adventure, and one has to go through that adventure in order to come to enlightenment. I have sometimes tried to describe this adventure as a *reductio ad absurdum* (carrying an absurdity to its extreme) of one's own false views. Buddhism is a process whereby the teacher makes you act consistently on your false views so that you come to find out for yourself that these views are false.

METHODS OF BUDDHISM
One might even say that Buddhism has nothing to teach, nothing whatever. Its purpose is simply to dissolve our illusions; awakening

ABOVE Buddhism teaches that all things are subject to change, that nothing is permanent... to counteract the wrong view that it was permanent.

happens only when the illusions have disappeared, just as the sun comes out when the clouds go away. But if you try to manufacture the sun before the clouds have dispersed, it will not be the real sun. Speculation – ideation, as such – does not lead to the awakening experience.

One of the methods Buddhist teachers use in dialogue is opposition or contradiction. People commonly say, for example, that Buddhism teaches that all things are subject to change, that nothing is permanent. Yet a subtler scholar may tell you that the Buddha taught that the world is impermanent in order to counteract the wrong view that it was permanent. Buddhist teachers always work through oppositions.

Student: 'What is the fundamental principle of Buddhism?'

Master: 'I have just finished washing the sauce pans.'

Conversely, if a person asks you a worldly question, you answer with a philosophical one:

Student: 'Please, will you pass me the knife?' The teacher passes it blade first. 'Please I want the other end.'

Master: 'What would you do with the other end?'

You see?

R.H. Blythe, a great student of Zen, was asked by some students, 'Do you believe in God?' He replied, 'If you do, I don't. If you don't, I do.' Thus when anything is taught, it is taught in order to counterbalance.

The Buddha taught that there was no self. Scholars have since debated what he meant. Was there was no ego in the sense of the

PREVIOUS SPREAD Buddhism

teaches… awakening

happens only when the

illusions have disappeared,

just as the sun comes out

when the clouds go away.

superficial 'I', centred on consciousness alone; or was there no self in the more classical Hindu sense of the *atman*, the ultimate self, the final reality, which is the root of all consciousness? Well, he may very well have denied the *atman* but perhaps with the idea of correcting something. If a person believes his basic self is beyond all vicissitude, he may believe in it as something to cling to, something that can give him a sense of security.

As long as you have a sense of security and you feel safe, you haven't got the point because it means you are still relying on something. A buddha is someone who doesn't depend on anything. That doesn't mean that they are strong in the sense of being tough. It means that they know very clearly that there isn't anything to depend on. The only thing to rely on is what you really are, but even that is not something you can hang on to. You can't catch hold of that and you don't need to: the sun doesn't need to shine a light on the sun.

That is what the teacher gets you to see by means of dialogue, opposition and paradox. He digs out all the dirt from underneath you, and you drop (or think you do) because you are used to having the earth there. But when you are fully floating in empty space, there is nowhere to drop. This is the meaning of

'thusness' or 'suchness'. People get a similar, marvellous feeling skin diving, when they get thirty feet below the surface and start to lose all sense of weight. They may have hours' worth of oxygen, but they suddenly realize that nothing matters, that everything is OK. They think, 'Supposing I do die – so what?' People have become so ecstatic that they have taken off their oxygen masks and presented them to the fish. In the same way, when Suzuki was asked what *satori* felt like, he said: 'It's just like ordinary everyday experience, except about two inches off the ground.'

LEVITATING MYSTICS

This sense of weightlessness is a peculiar state, and I do not mean that great mystics literally levitate. I mean it in the same way that we speak about the luminosity of mystical experience. Think of the vision of Giotto or Fra Angelico. They see light in everything – even shadows are full of colour.

You notice how full of light Picasso's work is, too. The mystic's vision of the world is always full of light. Only it isn't quite literal light. It isn't as if everything is blazing. Rather, everything is transparent, and that doesn't mean the mystic can see through your body to the wall or the other person behind.

Things are transparent because all has become clear. Problems the mystics once thought were the real problem have disappeared. I can't tell you how all becomes

clear, but it does. That is
what Zen means by
'thusness'. When things are
seen in the state of
'thusness', there are no
further problems about
them – they are what they
are and they do what they do.

When you finally arrive at the point where
you don't know what questions to ask any

more, the mystery clears up. The questions
have vanished – the problem has vanished.

The method of Buddhism effects a
transformation on the way you see things. I
would even say that it transforms the way you
sense them. In this respect, Buddhism is more
like ophthalmology than it is like religion. An
ophthalmologist corrects your vision so that
you see clearly. In exactly the same way, to
awaken is to see clearly. It is a transformation

of consciousness – but be careful of the implications of this phrase, because it doesn't necessarily mean an ecstatic, unnatural or even strange state of affairs.

By seeing clearly, I do not mean that you see everything in a different way, as if you had suddenly acquired the compound eyes of a fly and could see everything multiply. Everything is still the way it always has been, except it now has a completely different meaning. What we see, after all, depends on our point of view. We have been hypnotized by our own interpretations. To wake up is precisely to see everything just as it is, free of interpretation, evaluation or judgement.

There is a curious connection between experiencing this awakening and understanding it. This kind of understanding really has three steps. In the first place, there is an intellectual comprehension, the getting of an idea. Now what sort of idea do I mean? Let's take, for example, the awareness of a third dimension. If you look at things with one eye only, you don't see depth. But if you look with two eyes, the (third) dimension of depth appears. Once you have understood the concept of depth, though, you can see it.

Now, if I don't look at things with two eyes at once and look either with my left eye or with my right eye, I don't have binocular vision. But I still

see depth because I understand it to be there, and as a result of understanding it to be there, I see it. I couldn't understand the nature of depth if, looking at things, I was just told that they had two dimensions. But if I make an exploration and come to understand what a third dimension is, then I come to understand it more thoroughly and I'm quite clear about it. As a result of being clear about the third dimension, I see it.

In the same way, believe it or not, people at one time actually saw the crystal spheres in which the planets were supposed to be supported. Now how did they see these spheres if they were transparent? Well, they knew the spheres were up there. They were there for all to see because, naturally, you can always see through crystal. And people really do think like that: they see things they have been hypnotized into seeing. If you take away the suggestion, the belief, then they won't see it any more.

Conversely, if your number system only accounts '1–2–3 and many', as many cultures number systems have, you cannot see four things. You may see something that other people call 'four', but you won't see four, you will just see 'many'. Four is as many as five is many. You might even begin to have a concept of a little many, a middle many and a big many – and that's three again. So then it can never be a fact for a person like you that a room has four corners – it has either many corners or

just three. Once you embrace the idea
of four, however, you can see that a
room has four corners.

When I see the sun 'rising', I know that the
sun isn't moving; the earth is turning, and by
now I have travelled in enough aeroplanes to
see that for myself. So the question then is
this: if someone believes that the sun rises and
the earth stands still, when he looks at the
sunrise, does he see the same thing I see? I
don't think he does, because my seeing has an
entirely different interpretation from his
seeing, and in this way what he understands
determines what he sees.

In India 'yoga' means the method of
awakening through intellectual understanding.
People say you can't get it intellectually, which
is only partly true. For example, the old Hindu
saying, 'You cannot get wisdom through books'
is true because wisdom is a dialogue; but it
is also because books are only notes.

In other words, all sacred books are nothing
more than memoranda, just like the notation
of Hindu music is only a memorandum of the
raga. The musical notation is not something
you follow: it is a reminder of a certain raga or
theme, which you play and then improvise upon.

In the same way, all the aphorisms in the
Yoga-Sutra or the verses of the Bhagavad-Gita
are notes, little jottings, which the teacher will
explain. When something is understood
thoroughly by the thinking mind, it becomes a
sensation. As you truly understand it, you see.

When Buddhism envisages the character
and consciousness of the highest form of
human – the *bodhisattva* – it does not
describe somebody who is out of this world
or somebody who is in some weird state
of ecstasy or somebody who sees angels
everywhere. Real angels and gods are very
different from what you might suppose.
The dust is full of gods, if you really
look at dust; the pores of your skin
contain many universes.

How marvellous, to see that things are full
of gods! But you are still not seeing anything
different from the ordinary things you see; you
simply have a different understanding of it.
Nevertheless, you are still in the same everyday
life as everyone else.

THE BODHISATTVA

The *bodhisattva* is an extraordinarily
important vision for the whole of Asia,
because there has always been a tendency in
Asian spirituality to want to leave this world
and to escape. That is very understandable.
When life is rough and there are terrible
plagues and wars and hunger, people think,
'Oh, enough is enough. If we are going to be
reincarnated again and again into this mess,
isn't there some way of getting out?'

It is enough to cause you to lose all interest
in everyday life. Suppose you are a drunk, a
serious, dedicated drunk – lots of people are,
and they do this because they want to get out.

In this drunkenness they don't care whether they have no money, whether they are going to die, just so long as they can stay out. You might say (as many of us do), 'Well, that's very sad. Look at them wasting their lives.' But from their point of view, they are not wasting their lives at all. They are living the 'out' life they want to live.

A person may be an opium addict, and he will be in his special paradise. You say, 'Isn't that terrible?' Well, they want to be out, and they have made that decision. From their point of view, it is perfectly all right.

In their drugged state, they think that people who are pursuing those ends everybody else considers virtuous and practical are out of their minds. They may think, 'Why do all that? Why do you have to go on struggling and struggling to keep alive? What do you think all that effort is going to give you?'

So they may feel like it doesn't matter if it ends sooner or later, because time is an illusion. In this state of consciousness one can make a tiny bit of time into a long, long time. They may experience a hundred years in an afternoon.

Some even believe that you might have immortality through the fact that in the moment of your death, your sense of time expands infinitely. From the standpoint of an outside observer who is not in this state of consciousness, it may look as if some one is having their head cut off. But from the standpoint of the victim, the experience lasts forever because of the alteration of time's rhythms.

See how slippery philosophy can be?

Seek not to follow in the path of the Wise Ones.
Rather, seek that which they sought.

4

METATHINKING ON SUCHNESS

A RAFT FOR CROSSING
A RIVER

We have touched on various aspects of what might be called the 'religion of no religion' in which religion is often considered as a raft for crossing a river. And Zen Buddhism is a religion in the sense of a *dharma*, not so much a doctrine as a method. In this way religion is considered as the brick for knocking through the door or as a medicine to cure a sickness, which one discards after it has worked.

I have suggested that, in the Far East, this thinking culminated in a way of life in which, to a very large extent, the outward symptoms of religiousness disappear. This is especially true of the art forms in which the icon ceases to be a figure of a deity or a holy person and becomes simply a flowering branch, a rock, flowing water, clouds, birds or funny little old men.

This is a healthy sign because a curious thing occurs in the world of religious practice. The older a religion gets, the more the passage of time lends eminence to its original founders, and they become super-humans. The practice of the religion they founded becomes devoid of power, and its rituals sink into habit because people say, 'Well, we are living in a decadent age. In the past there were great heroes — Buddha, Jesus, Confucius,

LEFT Religion is considered as the brick for knocking through the door or as a medicine to cure a sickness, which one discards after it has worked.

Without going anywhere, you can know the whole world. Without even opening your window, you can know the ways of Heaven. You see, the further away you go, the less you know.

Muhammad and all their followers — and they did just marvellous things. But today everybody is rotten, so nobody can expect to get more than a little way along the path.'

I had a friend who went to India, and he was an astonishing fellow because he was so earnest. He would do anything; he was endowed with the power of self-discipline. After a while he had become the disciple of an Indian master who lived in this country. He became a vegetarian, practised yoga every day and was determined to get that great thing all of us want from gurus. Finally, his teacher told him the best place he could go to in all of India. So off he went. He joined a yoga school with a large faculty, where everybody was advanced in practising yoga. He became so earnest and so devoted that within four weeks he could do everything that the other students could, and many of them had been there two or three years.

My friend mastered all the physical postures and the breathing exercises and the concentration exercises. One day he said to one of the older students, 'Now what about real *samadhi*? Do you get that around here?'

The student said, 'No, none of us have got it yet. You had better ask the teachers.'

My friend began asking members of the faculty, 'What about *samadhi*? Do you get this in these parts?'

Most replied, 'No, not yet.'

'Well,' he said, 'I'm willing to spend any amount of time here. I don't have to get back, and I have just enough funds to get by, and so I am willing to do anything you tell me to and to practise with all my heart. Do any of you have *samadhi*?'

And they all told him, 'Well, no. Not yet.'

'Does anybody have it? Can you direct me to someone who does have it?'

'About 125 years ago there was someone who was really considered to have had it.'

My friend began to think, 'Why is it, then, that when the members of the faculty come out of their meditation period, they all look as if they have just had a good sleep? There is always the concept of a golden age to come, and maybe they are resting, and waiting for that.'

THUSNESS AND SUCHNESS

In the last chapter I tried to give you an idea of what is meant by 'thusness' or 'suchness', and we could also call this 'metathinking' or getting outside a situation to look at it. For example, if somebody who knows what the word 'tree' means teaches the meaning of 'tree' to another person, we say this is a meaningful communication because of the symbolism of the sign 'tree' for the physical entity. If we delve further, the question becomes, 'What is the meaning of the fact that these people can find and communicate meaning? What is the meaning of meaning?' We begin to unfold a very interesting situation in which all kinds of representations are coming into play, one way and another, but really, there is no one level at

The Wise don't just look at the surface, they also blow away the dust and drink the water. They don't just go for the flower but also the roots and fruit. Blow away the dust, now; come to the living water.

which one is preferable to any other.

In other words, 'suchness' or 'thusness' means coming into view of the world at a level where everything is equally meaningful or equally meaningless. The very notion of meaning at that level disappears. You may realize, then, that you have corresponding levels in yourself. Just as there is a level at which something is 'important' or 'unimportant' in the world, there is another level at which your problems of life and death are extremely important. But when you look at that level from another point of view – which you also have inside yourself – you will just see that 'I am the one who takes such things to be extremely important or unimportant'.

However, to have great concern about something is to put on a big show, and it requires a great expenditure of energy. Suppose you are concerned about people who are suffering. If you are going to try to correct that situation, you may put out a lot of energy and you go running around doing this, that and the other to help them out. And sometimes this will have the intended effect, but often it will not, and on occasion you will cause even more suffering as a result of your efforts. But looking at it in this larger context – which is, 'Here are people running around, stopping people from going this way and that way – which is itself a symptom of suffering' – you may discover that instead, you can go down and down inside yourself and come to a point where you see life simply as a phenomenon and not as a good life or a bad life.

PERCEPTION OF MAN

Still, 'thusness' is not a way of putting down the nature of things, and one of the aspects of 'thusness' is the consciousness involved. By its nature, 'thusness' is transparent and yet reverberating. Within this domain there is room for an enormous number of value games, but you must remember that value games are only games. We have got into the habit of thinking of the world as a physical continuum – in fact, not even as a continuum. We divide the universe into the inert and the 'ert', the conscious and the unconscious, the living and the dead, the organic and the inorganic. The mythology of the nineteenth century dictated that everything was essentially inorganic and that consciousness was ultimately purely mineral and metallic. People believed that everything was very complicated, with all kinds of liquids and gooey things, but that once magnified everything was made up of minerals, which are fundamentally a form of machinery.

Now, my objection to that point of view is simply that it's a way of looking down your nose at things. In fact, objectivity is itself an objection. We won't go into such embarrassing questions as 'Who objects?' but

If you know what it is, don't talk it away: if you do, then you don't understand. Hush, keep it in, and your doorway shut. Steer clear of sharpness and untangle the knots. Feel your lightness and let it merge with others.

when you construe the whole universe in an objectionable way, you are really saying: 'I want to be miserable.' You are, of course, perfectly entitled to be miserable. Another version is, 'I want to be realistic,' which is also miserable in a sense, and that's perfectly OK, too, if that is the way you want to be. But if you state that you want to be realistic, you have absolutely no right to say that your viewpoint is more valid than ours when we say the opposite, because both are really opinions.

Actually, the universe is a continuum of whatever it is, a kind of encompassing 'thusness', and life is a spectrum in which there are the very conscious things and the only slightly conscious things. All of it, however, is conscious on some level, and this is logical if

ABOVE When you ring a
bell, your ears receive it as
'ding!' and the bell
experiences a state of
vibration, which is a simple
form of consciousness.

you think that life is made up of minerals. When you ring a bell, your ears receive it as 'ding!' and the bell experiences a state of vibration, which is a very simple form of consciousness, but consciousness nevertheless. With this understanding, you don't have to grapple with the dilemma of how consciousness got into a mechanical world in the first place. It is apparent that it has always been there, and that everything is conscious, although in differing degrees.

The idea of a spectrum of consciousness seems far more plausible than the idea of having two completely different substances, one called 'matter', and another called 'spirit' or perhaps 'mind'. If you see, for example, a beautiful fern, you might begin by saying, 'Here is a stalk, just an isolated thing.' You might then observe more stalks coming out of the sides of the main one, and then from these stalks grow even more stalks. So you observe:

PREVIOUS SPREAD If you see a beautiful fern, you might begin by saying, 'Here is a stalk, just an isolated thing.' You might then observe more stalks.

'Well, look at that. It's getting very spiky isn't it? Full of little spines.' Finally, gradually, right on the edge of the spines the stalks become soft and hairy. Suddenly, you have what you'd call a vegetable.

Take another example. Some people have extremely modern watches – that is to say designer watches with marks instead of numbers. There are watches with just four spots on them – at twelve and six o'clock, nine and three o'clock. On the other hand, you can buy very expensive watches that can do all kinds of involved things: serve as stopwatches, tell you the date and even include tachometers. The calibrations of a watch like this can become so complex that it can begin to look like the details of a flower. What started out looking like a simple metal object ends up taking on the appearance of a wonderful growing, alive thing. Once you reach some mysterious point of complexity, an 'object' seems to come to life. And this is one example of what I mean by a spectrum of consciousness.

SAYING YES TO THE 'ERT'

Now, whether you say that the inert is merely less alive or that the alive is merely the maximum complexity of the inert really depends on whether you want to say 'yes' to the world or whether you want to say 'no'.

A great square has no corners.
A great work is never done with.
A great shout comes from a whisper, and the greatest of forms is beyond shape.
Tao without substance, invisible, ever-creating. Forever creating.

Saying 'yes' makes everything come alive; saying 'no' makes everything seem dead.

When you say 'no' and it all seems dead, what happens? You experience an extreme form of differentiation between yourself, on the one hand, and everything that you experience on the other. This is what happens when you objectify the world. If you say 'no' to life in this way, you have to say 'no' to yourself as well because it follows that if the world is junk, then so must you be. Therefore, the only way to sustain that view and maintain your own credibility as well is to separate yourself from the world.

RIGHT The calibrations of a watch can become so complex that it can begin to look like a flower... taking on the appearance of a wonderful growing thing.

However, when you appreciate the world – when you say 'yes' to it – you involve yourself with it and you don't stand aside from it any longer. You admit that you, too, are part of the whole thing, and your ego, your self, is so inextricably involved with everything that you experience no ultimate difference between you and what is going on around you. At this point, you have discovered a total system. You are one with it; you are not standing aside from it.

This is not easy to grasp for those of us whose thinking is based on sentence structure and grammar, with their subjects, verbs and objects. Somehow, we have to get behind language to experience the totality of life and consciousness. A limerick I made up points to our dilemma:

There was a young man who said though
It seems that I know that I know,
What I'd like to see
Is the I that knows me
When I know that I know that I know.

The young man in the limerick experiences life as a hall of mirrors. Yet when you see that, the physical world and consciousness are inseparable and the physical world is no longer reflected in the mirror of consciousness; it and consciousness are all one. What you are seeing 'out there', in front of you, is actually a sensation inside your head; it is all a conversion of quanta in the external world that forms in your brain.

Thirty spokes on a cartwheel go towards the hub that is the centre — but look, there is nothing at the centre and that is precisely why it works!

Your brain in its turn can seem to be something in the external world, and you may have the sensation that somebody standing inside your brain is looking at the reflected image of the external world, saying: 'Well, there it is. What a nice picture.' The centres of the optic nerves are right in the back of your head, and so what you are seeing in front of your eyes is right back in here where it is actually happening.

Yet there isn't really somebody in the middle who is turning around to look at the back of your head to see what's out in front. The sensation of your self and the sensation of other people are the same thing. That is mutual between all of us. We all have our view of other people and other things: views of views and views of viewings. So you don't have to introduce the problem of how the knower knows. You don't have to wonder how the world makes an impact on the knowing subject

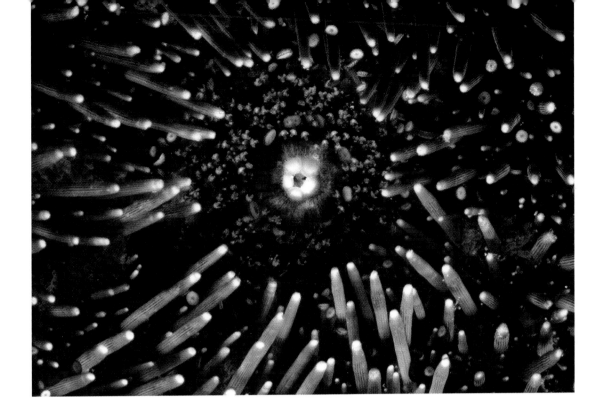

ABOVE Your head and eyes are points… like so many sensitive hairs, like a sea urchin with all those little spines coming out, and each of us is one of these spines.

so that the subject can be aware of – be conscious of – everything else. That kind of mirror or camera process isn't necessary to what is going on.

This is important to understand, because everybody's thought is so powerfully influenced by these metaphors, the metaphors that liken knowing and consciousness to mirrors or cameras. These metaphors introduce unnecessary complications.

What you are aware of in terms of external sensory experiences, in terms of so-called internal feelings, internal thoughts: that is what you are. Krishnamurti puts it so beautifully when he tells the reader that behind the stream of thoughts there isn't a thinker. He says, you create the thinker. You create the

thought of a thinker behind the thoughts in a moment of insecurity, when you want to withdraw. In reality, there is simply the existence of what you might call 'luminous experience'. And you can take away the word 'luminous' and put the word 'conscious' in its place.

Your head, your nervous system, your eyes, your senses and your body – these do not encounter the external environment from outside of it. You are the external environment. Rather, your head and eyes are points, manifested by the environment as a whole, as a totality through which it feels all around, like so many sensitive hairs, like a sea urchin with all those little spines coming out of it, and each of us is one of these spines.

NEXT PAGE You may have the sensation that somebody standing inside your brain is looking at the reflected image of the external world.

The world spans out in four directions. Can you be as embracing?
Birthing, nurturing, sustaining; The Tao does this unceasingly.

5
JUST SO – I:
THE GOLDEN AGE OF ZEN

THE HOAX OF TELLING

A lecture on Zen is always something like a hoax because it really deals with a domain of experience that cannot be talked about. But at the same time, one must remember that nothing can really be talked about adequately, and the whole art of poetry is to say what cannot be said. So every poet, every artist, when he gets to the end of his work, feels that he has left out something absolutely essential. Zen has always described itself as a finger pointing at the moon. We must be very careful not to mistake the finger for the moon, and especially careful (if the finger looks religious) not to suck on it for comfort instead of following where it points.

In the Sanskrit saying *tat tvam asi* ('that art thou') Zen is concerned with 'that'. 'That' is the word used for brahman, the absolute reality in Hindu philosophy. You are 'that', only in disguise – disguised so well that you have forgotten it. But unfortunately, ideas like the ultimate ground of being, the self, brahman, ultimate reality, the great void – all that is very abstract talk. Zen has a much more direct way of coming to an understanding of 'thatness' as it is called, or *tathata* in Sanskrit. Zen has been summed up in these four statements:

* It has no dependence on words or letters.

* It is a direct

The Tao is the breath that never dies. Mother to all Creation. It is the root and ground of every soul – the fountain of Heaven and Earth, laid open.

transmission outside scriptures, apart from tradition.

* It is a direct pointing to the human mind.

* It is seeing into one's own nature and becoming a buddha, becoming enlightened and being awakened from the normal hypnosis to which almost all of us are subject.

I think that one reason Zen appeals to Westerners lies in its unusual quality of humour. As a rule, religions are not humorous. Religions are serious. When one looks at Zen art and reads Zen stories, it is quite apparent that something here is not serious in the ordinary sense, no matter how sincere the content may be. Another aspect that appeals to Westerners is that Zen has no doctrines. There is nothing you have to believe; it does not moralize. In fact, Zen is not particularly concerned with morals at all. It is a field of inquiry, rather like physics.

Teachers in the West present a kind of Zen that is different from that which you will find today in Japan. From Dr Suzuki on, Zen masters in America have essentially presented early Chinese Zen from the old writings (ranging from shortly before 700 CE to 1000 CE). Early Chinese Zen has a very different flavour from modern Japanese Zen. Many of the people who go to Japan to study Zen thoroughly disapprove of Dr Suzuki and also, naturally, of my exposition of Zen, because we do not make a great fetish of studying Zen by sitting. Zen can be practised in one situation in Japan today: one sits and one sits and one sits. R.H. Blythe once asked a Zen master, 'What would you do if you had only one half-hour to live?' And he said, 'I would do *zazen*,' which means he would sit like a buddha and practise meditation. Blythe had given him several choices: Would you listen to your favourite music? Would you have a dinner? Would you get drunk? Would you like the company of a beautiful woman? Would you take a walk? What would you do? Or would you just go on with your daily business as if nothing was going to happen? In other words, would you wind up your watch? So Blythe was disappointed in this answer, and he said: 'You know, sitting is only one way of doing Zen.'

Buddhism speaks of the Four Dignities of Man – walking, standing, sitting and lying. *Zazen* is simply the Japanese word for 'sitting Zen', and, of course, there must also be walking Zen, standing Zen and lying Zen. You should know, for example, how to sleep in a Zen way – which means to sleep thoroughly. Zen can be described as: 'When hungry, eat. When tired, sleep.' When one student heard that description, he asked, 'Doesn't everybody do that?' The master said, 'They don't. When hungry they don't just eat, they think of ten thousand things. When tired they don't just sleep, they dream innumerable dreams.'

So in a sense, this sounds like the old Western truism: 'Whatever your hand finds to do, do it with all your might.' But that is not the same thing as Zen, though many people like to sum up Zen in that way. A famous story beautifully illustrates the current relationship between East and West. Paul Reps, who drew a lovely book called Zen Telegrams, once asked a Zen master to sum up Buddhism in one phrase. The master said: 'Don't act, bad act.' Reps was simply delighted, because he thought the master had said: 'Don't act, but act.'

That, of course, would describe the Taoist principle of *wu-wei*, action in the spirit of not being separate from the world. Realizing fully that you are also the universe, your action on it is not an interference but an expression of the totality. But the master's English was very bad, and Paul Reps had misunderstood him. The master had said 'Don't act, bad act', and this is the sort of attitude that all clergy have developed over the centuries. You know how it is when you go to church (if you do). The sermon often boils down to: 'My dear people, you ought to be good.' Everybody knows they ought to be good, but hardly anybody knows how – or even what 'good' is.

SUDDEN ZEN

The real fascination of Zen for the West, however, is that it promises a sudden insight

If you mould a cup you have to make a hollow: it is the emptiness within it that makes it useful. In a house it is the empty spaces – the doors, the windows – that make it useable. Without their nothingness they would be nothing.

into something that is supposed to take a very long time. Psychoanalysts will tell you that the troubles you have got yourself into over the years cannot be undone in a day and that it will take many, many sessions – maybe twice a week for several years – for you to get straightened out. Christians tell you that to embark on a path of spiritual discipline you must find a spiritual director and submit yourself to the will of God but you may not attain the high states of contemplative prayer for very many years. Hindus and Buddhists also say it will require many long years – perhaps many incarnations – of meditation, hard concentration, difficult practice and stern discipline. Yet when the artist Sabro Hasegawa was asked how long it would take to awaken

through Zen, he said, 'It may take you three seconds. It may take you thirty years.'

Zen literature abounds with stories in which there is a dialogue, a non-rational exchange of questions and answers, between a Zen teacher and his student. Often, at the end of this swift interchange, the student seems to get the point. And sometimes he does not. I once gave a book of these dialogues to a friend who was deeply interested in Eastern philosophy. He later told me: 'I have not understood a word, but it has cheered me up enormously.' This book is called the Mumonkan (in Chinese, Wu-men-kuan), which means 'The Barrier with no Gate' or 'The Gateless Gate'.

In one of its stories, a student said to the master Joshu, 'I have been in this monastery for some time, and I have had no instruction from you.'

The master asked him, 'Have you had breakfast?'

'Yes.'

'Then go wash your bowl.'

And the monk was awakened. Now you may think that the bowl is a symbol of the great void, the all-containing universe. And the monk had probably washed it earlier, because in a monastery, immediately after eating, the monks pour tea into the bowl, swill it around, wash it and wipe it out. In that case,

you might think that the master was saying 'Don't gild the lily' or, to use a really Zen phrase, 'Don't put legs on a snake or a beard on a eunuch'.

The point of that story is so clear, however, that its very simplicity makes it difficult. In this sense, all these stories resemble jokes. A joke is told to make you laugh: the punch-line has an immediate impact. When you get the point of a joke you laugh spontaneously, but if the point has to be explained to you, you do not laugh so readily – you force a laugh. In exactly the same way, these stories are intended to generate a sudden insight into the nature of being. 'Nature of being' again sounds very abstract. What the teacher actually said was 'go wash your bowl'.

NOT THIS, NOT THAT

Bodhidharma, who brought Buddhism to China, always insisted that he had nothing to teach. So why did he come? That is one of the fundamental questions. I have often said when I am giving a lecture that I am not trying to persuade anyone to believe a certain point of view. In fact, I have nothing to tell anyone; were I to presume that I did, it would be like picking someone's pocket and then selling them their own watch. You might wonder, then, why I talk or write. But you might just as well ask the sky why it is blue, or the clouds why they float around, or the birds why they sing.

In a great Zen story, one of the old masters

said: 'When I was a young man and knew nothing of Buddhism, mountains were mountains, and waters were waters. But once I began to understand a little Buddhism, mountains were no longer mountains, and waters no longer waters.'

In other words, when one starts scientific and philosophical inquiries, everything is explained away in terms of its causes. But if one follows this line of reasoning carefully, one sees that all the apparently separate things in the world are in reality not separate at all.

Finally, in much this way, the master came to understand that 'mountains were mountains, and waters are waters'.

Zen calls this 'direct pointing'. It is not

The Tao that can be talked about is not the true Tao. The name that can be named is not the true Name. Everything in the universe comes out of Nothing.

asserting that you need to be able to see the world without forming ideas about it. That would be going too far; yet it is, nevertheless, a movement in the right direction. Zen teachers speak of the virtue of what they call *mushin* ('no mind') or *munin* ('no thought'). This is not an anti-intellectual attitude, and *munin* does not mean not having any thoughts at all.

The ordinary person is just as bamboozled by thinking as the university professor; you can think intellectually in an analytical way. *Munin* means not to be fooled by thoughts; not to be hypnotized by the forms of speech and images that we have for the world; not to be hypnotized into thinking that this is the way the world really is.

Do not let words limit the possibilities of life. I own a fan with an inscription on it written by a hundred-year-old Zen master. The inscription says, 'I don't understand – I don't know anything about it.'

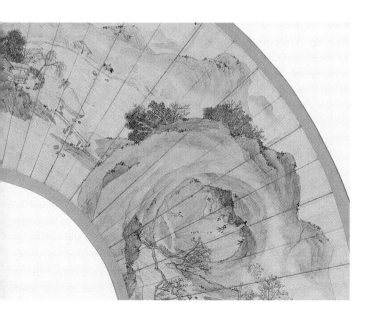

BELOW I own a fan with an inscription on it written by a hundred-year-old Zen master. The inscription says, 'I don't understand – I don't know anything about it.'

BODHIDHARMA NOT KNOWING

When Bodhidharma first came to China a little before 500 CE he was interviewed by Emperor Wu, a great patron of Buddhism. The emperor said: 'We have caused many monasteries to be built, monks and nuns to be ordained, and the scriptures to be translated into Chinese. What is the merit of this?'

Bodhidharma replied, 'No merit whatever.'

Well, the popular understanding of Buddhism was that doing good things, religious things like that, acquired merit for you. Merit led you to better and better in future lives so that you could eventually become liberated. So the emperor was completely set back by this answer. He said, 'What, then, is the first principle of the holy doctrine?'

Bodhidharma told him, 'Vast emptiness and nothing holy.' Or, 'In vast emptiness there is nothing holy.'

The emperor demanded, 'Who is it then that stands before us?' He was implying, 'Aren't you supposed to be a holy man?'

And Bodhidharma said, 'I don't know.'

So the poem reads:

> *Plucking flowers to which the butterflies come*
> *Bodhidharma says I don't know.*

And another poem:

> *If you want to know where the flowers come from*
> *Even the God of Spring doesn't know.*

Anybody who says he knows what Zen is, is a fraud. Nobody knows. You don't know who you are. To know who you are is to be able to smell your own nose. This is why, when I discussed the text called Shobo-genzo ('Treasure Chamber of the Eye of True Dharma' by Dogen) with a Zen master in Japan, he said: 'That is a terrible book. It explains everything so clearly. It gives the show away.' You don't need any book for Zen. The sound of the rain needs no translation.

ZEN IN THE PERSPECTIVE OF HISTORY

Zen is a subdivision of Mahayana Buddhism, the school of Buddhism concerned with realizing buddha-nature in this world, but not by going off to the mountains or by renouncing family life, everyday life, as if it were an entanglement. The ideal figure of Mahayana Buddhism is the *bodhisattva*, somebody who has attained nirvana, but instead of disappearing comes back in many guises. *Bodhisattvas* in Zen art are often represented as bums. There is even a famous painting of one *bodhisattva* in the form of a prostitute. The artist Sengei painted a beautiful one of the bum Hotei (Pu-tai in Chinese), who is always immensely fat. Hotei is saying:

ABOVE The bum Hotei is always immensely fat. Hotei is saying: 'Buddha is dead... I just had a wonderful sleep and didn't even dream about Confucius.'

'Buddha is dead. Maitreya [the next Buddha] hasn't come yet. I just had a wonderful sleep and didn't even dream about Confucius.' He is stretching and yawning as he wakes.

Zen is what became of Indian Mahayana Buddhism when it entered China and was deeply influenced by Taoism and Confucianism. Zen monks then brought Confucian ideas to Japan. The origins of Zen begin around the year 414 CE, when a great Hindu scholar, Kumarajiva, and his assistants were translating the sutras into Chinese. One of Kumarajiva's students taught that all beings have the capacity to become buddhas, to become enlightened — even rocks and stones. Even heretics and evil-doers have the buddha-nature or buddha-potential in them. Everybody said this student was a dreadful heretic himself, of course, but then a text called the Nirvana-Sutra arrived from India, and it said precisely the same thing. So everyone had to admit that this man was right. The assistant then began to teach that awakening must be instantaneous, a kind of all-or-nothing state. I do not mean that the state doesn't have degrees of intensity.

Once you see the principle, however, you see the whole thing. When the bottom falls out of the bucket, as they say, all the water goes at once.

So these men promulgated the way of sudden awakening. Bodhidharma came later, and, according to legend, he was the first of a line of six patriarchs. The second, named Eka (Hui-k'o), had formerly been an army general. Sosan (in Chinese, Seng-ts'an), the third, wrote Shinjinmei (in Chinese, Hsin-hsin-ming), which is a marvellous little summary of Buddhism in verse. And so on until they came to E'no (Huineng), the sixth patriarch, who died in 713 CE. E'no was the real founder of Chinese Zen, a man who synthesized the whole practice. His collected discourses are contained in the Platform Sutra, which every student of Zen should read.

E'no really fused Zen with the Chinese way of doing things. He emphasized that it is a mistake to think that you can attain buddhahood by sitting down all day and keeping your mind blank. Many students at that time practised *dhyana*, the Hindu practice of sitting still in contemplation for long periods. The Sanskrit word *dhyana* became Chan in Chinese, which in turn became Zen in Japanese. At the time, everybody thought the proper way to contemplate was to be as still as possible.

But according to Zen, being still is to be a stone buddha rather than a living buddha. I can knock a stone buddha on the head – clunk! – and it has no feelings.

The famous Zen master named Tanka once went to a little lonely temple on a freezing cold night. He took one of the statues of the Buddha off the altar, split it up, and made a fire. When the temple attendant arrived in the morning, he was horrified at the broken image. Tanka took his stick and started raking the ashes. The temple priest asked, 'What are you looking for?'

Tanka replied, 'I am looking for the *sali* [the jewels that are supposed to be found in the body of a genuine buddha when he is cremated].'

So the priest said, 'You can't expect to find sali from a wooden buddha.'

'In that case,' said Tanka, 'Let me have the other buddha for my fire.'

That, you see, is the difference between a living buddha and a stone buddha. As far as Zen is concerned, a person who thinks that to be awakened you must have no emotions, no feelings – you couldn't possibly lose your temper, feel annoyed or get depressed – doesn't have the right idea at all. 'If that is your ideal,' said E'no, 'You might just as well be a block of wood or a piece of stone.'

And what do most people do? They go looking for fool's gold and auspicious signs. Only, you see, I am lazy and I don't give a damn for fame or money. I am like a child who can't bring himself to smile.

While all those emotions are going on, your real mind is imperturbable, just like the sky. When you move your hand through the sky, you don't leave a trace. The birds don't stain the blue when they pass by. When a pool of water reflects the image of a flock of geese, the reflection doesn't remain.

BEING PURE-MINDED

So, to be pure-minded – or clear-minded – in the Zen way it is not important to have no thoughts; nor is it a question of avoiding dirty thoughts. One great master of the Tang dynasty, when asked 'What is buddha?' answered 'A dry turd'. Purity, in Zen, means that your mind does not stick to anything. You don't harbour grievances. You are not attached

PREVIOUS SPREAD The birds
don't stain the blue when
they pass by. When a pool
of water reflects the image
of a flock of geese, the
reflection doesn't remain.

to the past. You go with
life, which is flowing all
the time: that is the Tao,
the flow of life. You are
flowing along with it
whether you want to or
not. You can swim against
the stream, but you will still be moved along
by it, and all you eventually do is wear yourself
out in futility. Yet if you swim with the stream,
the whole strength of the stream is yours.
Of course, the difficulty that so many of us
have is finding out which way the stream is
going, but certainly, as it goes, all of the
past vanishes; the future has not yet arrived.
There is only one place to be – here
and now. Nor is there any way of being
somewhere else. If you understand that
thoroughly, your task is finished. You
become instantaneous, momentous.

This was E'no's principle. He left five great
disciples who taught essentially the same thing.
But these disciples had disciples, and those
disciples had disciples – and lineages
developed. Zen broke into five houses, some of
which have not endured. Zen continued on in
two main forms, the
Japanese Rinzaizen, after
the great master Rinzai
Lin-chi, who lived towards
the end of the ninth
century, and the Soto
school. The two schools

LEFT You go with life,
which is flowing all the
time: that is the Tao, the
flow of life. You are
flowing along with it
whether you want to or not.

*The softest thing can ride like a
galloping horse through the hardest
of things. Like water penetrating
rock. So the invisible enters in.
That is why I know it is wise to
act by doing nothing. How few,
how very few understand this.*

have slightly different emphases: Soto is more
serene in its approach, Rinzai more gutsy.
Rinzai people use the koan method; Soto
people don't – at least not in the same way.

The period between the death of the sixth
patriarch, E'no, and the year 1000 CE is
considered the golden age of Zen. After these
formative years, Zen began to decline in China.
It became mixed up with other forms of
Buddhism and suffered the fate of most other
spiritual disciplines: it was side-tracked into
occult and psychic matters and began
emphasizing the development of paranormal
powers. It also became involved with Chinese
(Taoistic) alchemy and all sorts of foolishness
that, for essential Zen, is beside the point.
However, a very strong strain of Zen went to

Japan, first in 1130 with the monk Eisei, and then c.1200 with Dogen, who founded the great monastery at Eihei-ji, which exists to this day.

In this golden age of Chinese Zen, the main method of study was walking Zen rather than sitting Zen (zazen). All monks were great travellers. They walked for miles through fields and mountains, visiting temples to see if they could find a master who would cause their spark to flash.

They wanted to get what is called in Mandarin wu (in Japanese, satori), to awaken from the illusion of being a separate ego, locked up in a bag of skin, and to discover that one is the whole universe.

A great tree that takes a

crowd to span its base,

started from being a tiny seed.

A tower nine levels high

began deep in the ground.

A journey of a thousand miles

starts with but a single step.

WHO'S CARRYING MY CORPSE?

One of the koans, or meditation problems of Zen, asks this question: 'Who is it that is carrying your corpse around?' Find that fellow. Find out who the thinker is behind the thoughts. Who is the genuine you? One of the methods used for this is shouting. The Zen master says to his student: 'Now, I want to hear you. I want to hear you say the word "move" and really mean it. Because I want to hear not just the sound, but also the person who says it. Now produce that for me.'

So the student says, 'Move.'

And the Zen teacher says, 'No, no, not yet.' 'Move.'

And the teacher responds, 'It's only coming from your throat. I want to hear your belly, now.'

The trick is, you see, that it will never come while the person is trying to differentiate between a true 'move' and a false 'move'. You have to act with confidence; you just do it. But since people are not used to that, it is necessary to set up protected situations in which they can act. Zen training creates enclosures in which this behaviour can be practised until people become experts and know how to apply it in all situations. So a Zen teacher puts his students in all kinds of situations where, in the normal course of social relations, they would get stuck – by asking nonsense questions, by making absurd remarks and by all kinds of unhinging

techniques. Above all, the master keeps them stirred up with impossible demands: to hear the sound of one hand clapping, to stop the sound of a train whistle in the distance, to take the four divisions of Tokyo out of one's sleeve, to take Mount Fuji out of a pillbox.

They ask all these impossible questions to unglue us from our habitual modes of perception and to help us realize that it would be just as good a game to drop dead as to go on living. Is a lightning flash bad because it lives for a second compared to the sun, which endures for billions of years? You can't make that sort of comparison: long-lived creatures and short-lived creatures are part of the same world. That is the meaning of the saying, 'Flowering branches grow naturally, some short, some long.'

BEHAVING ZEN

In a Zen community spontaneous behaviour is encouraged – within certain limits. As the student becomes more and more used to these limits, they are expanded, until eventually he can be trusted to go out on the street and behave like a true Zen character. The important thing is to remember that you can't make any mistakes – after all, what are mistakes? Now, from childhood we have had to conform to a certain social game. If you conform to this game, you can make mistakes

PREVIOUS SPREAD

… to stop the sound of a train whistle in the distance, to take the four divisions of Tokyo out of one's sleeve, to take Mount Fuji out of a pillbox.

or not make mistakes. This thought pattern thing is going on in us at all times: 'You must do the right thing. A certain conduct is appropriate here, a certain conduct is appropriate there.' That gives us a double-self all our lives, and we never grow up. The whole of life plays a game, a childhood game. We are in a constant state of competition: 'I'm stronger than you,' 'I'm wiser than you,' 'I'm more loving than you,' 'I'm more sophisticated than you.' In terms of that competition we can, of course, lose face and in that context make mistakes.

But a Zen student, a true monk, is a person who is not involved with the status game. And to be a master, one must arrive at the point where they are not trying to be a master. From the Zen point of view, being 'better than anybody else' simply doesn't make any sense – it is a totally meaningless concept because you can see every person is manifesting the

ABOVE When you are tired of playing a certain kind of game, you are as naturally flowing in another direction as a tree putting out a new branch.

marvel of the universe in the same way as the stars, the water, the winds and the animals. You see all things as being in the right place, unable to make mistakes – although they may think they are making or not making mistakes and playing all these competitive games.

ZEN GAMES

Now when the game begins to bore you, or give you ulcers, then you at last raise the question of how to get out of it. You become interested in things like Zen – and this is simply a symptom of your growing in a certain direction. When you are tired of playing a certain kind of game, you are as naturally flowing in another direction as a tree putting out a new branch. But remember, in the process of growth the oak is not better than the acorn. What does the oak do? It produces acorns. Or, as I love to say, a chicken is one egg's way of becoming other eggs. So an oak is an acorn's way of becoming other acorns.

The real reason that Zen cannot be explained is that you have to make a jump from the valuation game – of better people versus worse people, of 'in' groups versus 'out' groups – by discovering that they all are mutually interdependent. When you see that and you aren't in competition, then you don't make a mistake because you don't dither. You would think that the Zen master as we know him might contradict this interdependent view of life. He might appear to be a very superior, authoritarian figure. He deliberately comes on like that at the beginning and puts up a terrific show of being an awful dragon, and this screens out all sorts of people who don't have the nerve to get into the work.

But once you are in, an odd change takes place – the master becomes the brother. He becomes an affectionate helper to all his students, and they love him as they would a brother, rather than respect him as they would a father. The students and masters make jokes about each other. They have a curious kind of social relationship: although it has all the outward trappings of being authoritarian, everybody knows on the inside that the show is a joke. Liberated people have to be very cool, otherwise, in a society that doesn't believe in equality (and cannot possibly practise it), they would be considered extremely subversive. So great Zen masters wear purple and gold, carry sceptres and sit on thrones, and all this is done to cool it. And in this way the outside world knows the Zen practitioners are all right: they have discipline, they have order, so they won't upset the social status quo.

The Tao gives without holding on to what it has made.
It gives everything essence, without reward.

6

JUST SO – II: THE JAPANESE
MONASTIC TRADITION

HAVING DISCUSSED the basic principles of Zen, I will now pass on to the more practical side of it by discussing Zen monastic training.

A Zen monastery is not a monastery in the Christian sense because it practises more than it teaches. A typical institution consists of a campus, and on the campus are many buildings. Around the edges of Japanese monasteries you will invariably find independent temples founded in times past by noble families, because one of the things the Buddhists did when they came to the Far East was to exploit ancestor worship, the great religion of China, and this endeared then to the upper classes. The Buddhist priests performed services (much like requiem masses) to ensure the repose of souls or to pray for good reincarnations for one's ancestors. Buddhist memorial services for the departed are among the principle functions of temples in Japan.

People don't go to temple in the same way that Westerners go to church; they make pilgrimages to temples. At a great temple, such as Eihei-ji, you will find on almost any morning about 500 people attending the 4 o'clock 'service' or chanting the Buddhist scriptures. Temples conduct special services, such as memorial services, weddings and all kinds of funerals.

LEFT The sangha hall, or sodo, is the centre of the temple… a long, spacious room with platforms on both sides and a wide passage down the centre.

Those who understand appear as if they do not; those who do not understand pretend that they do. This is what it means to be flawed. But the Wise One is sick of all faults. He is sick of being sick. He is well.

However, they don't have a parish community as we find it in Christianity.

The heart of the Zen temple is the *sodo*. *So* is Japanese for the *sangha*, a Sanskrit word that means the 'followers of the Buddha'. *Do* simply means hall. So the *sangha* hall, or *sodo*, is the centre of the temple. It consists of a number of rooms, but the main one, the actual *sodo* itself, is a long, spacious room with platforms on both sides and a wide passage down the centre. Each six-foot-wide platform contains a number of *tatami* mats that measure six feet by three feet. Each monk is assigned a mat. Against the wall on a shelf behind the mat, he stores all his possessions (which are very simple). The mat is the monk's sleeping place and his meditation place.

An image of Manjushri stands in the hall, more or less in the centre of the passage between the platforms. *Manjushri* is a *bodhisattva* – they call him *Manju* in Japan – and in his hand he holds the sword of wisdom, *prajna*, which cuts asunder all illusions.

The monasteries also have kitchens, libraries and special temples for services. Other buildings are the quarters of the *honshi* (the abbot, the administrative head of the temple) and the quarters of the *roshi* (its spiritual teacher). In the Rinzai school of Zen, every temple is independent – there are no popes, no archbishops – though there is a fraternal relationship between all the temples of the sect. The Soto sect has some hierarchy, but still, on the whole, the *honshi* is the person in charge. The *roshi* is the respected teacher, the man everybody is terrified of, at least on the outside.

REPELLENT ZEN

If you want to study in one of these institutions, beware – the monasteries make it difficult. Unlike the welcome attitude you find in Christian churches, here they repel you. Westerners, of course, are treated with a courtesy that is not ordinarily accorded to the Japanese. The reason for this is that the monks realize that a Westerner who has taken the trouble to learn Japanese, to get himself over the oceans and to live under unfamiliar conditions is certainly pretty serious about Zen.

By tradition, you arrive at the gate in your travelling gear. The Zen monk's travelling gear is most picturesque. He wears a great mushroom on his head, an enormous straw hat; a black robe, shorter than a kimono, with long white tabi socks underneath; and geta, the wooden sandals on bridges that raise you up a bit. The travelling monk carries on his front a little box in which he stores his eating bowls, his razor, his toothbrush and such necessities of life. When he arrives he is told that the monastery is very poor, and they can't afford to take in any more students; the teacher is getting old and it might tax his strength; and so on. So he has to sit on the steps. He puts his travelling box in front of him, takes off his big hat, lays his head on the box and waits there all day. He is invited in for meals to a special little guesthouse because no travelling monk can be refused hospitality. He is admitted at night into this special place, but he is expected not to sleep but to spend all night in meditation. In the past, this treatment lasted for a week to ten days in order to test this fellow out.

Finally, the assistant to the *roshi* comes and tells him that the roshi will talk to him. To a young monk, the *roshi* would be a formidable fellow, usually an older man with an indefinable strength – a certain fierceness coupled with tremendous directness; somebody who sees right through you. By his very presence he asks this young fellow

what he wants, why he has come.

'I came to be instructed in Zen,' the monk hesitatingly offers.

The teacher replies, 'Well we don't teach anything here. There isn't anything in Zen to study.'

The student knows – or thinks he knows – that this 'not anything' studied in Zen is the real thing. As a Buddhist he knows that what 'isn't anything' is the universe, the great void, the *shunyata*, and so he isn't fazed. He says, 'Nevertheless, you do have people who are working here and meditating under your instruction, and I'd like to join them.'

'Well, maybe,' says the *roshi*, 'But strictly on probation.' Then the monks note all the details, and the noviciate pays a ridiculously small fee to be able to stay – it is very inexpensive. Soon the teacher comes back and says, 'Now, why do you want to study Zen?'

'Because I'm oppressed by the rounds of birth and death, by the vicious circles of life in

ABOVE The Zen monk's travelling gear is picturesque. He wears a great mushroom on his head, an enormous straw hat; a black robe, shorter than a kimono.

which I find myself, by suffering, by pain and so on. I want to be emancipated.'

The *roshi* then inquires, 'Who is it that wants to be emancipated?'

And that's a stopper.

There's a good old story about one of these preliminary interviews. The master starts off with very casual questions: 'Where is your home town? What's your name? What did your father do? Where did you go to college? Why is my hand so much like the Buddha's hand?' And suddenly, in mid-conversation – clunk, the student is blocked. Essentially, the basic question, or koan, is, 'Who are you? What is it that wants to escape from birth and death? I won't take words for an answer. I want to see you, and all you are showing me at the moment is your mask.'

So then the student is sent back to the monk's quarters, where he is taught how to behave, what the rules are, how to eat and how to meditate. In Zen they sit on a padded cushion about the thickness of a telephone directory, which would be an admirable substitute. With their legs crossed in the lotus posture and with their feet resting on the thighs (like statues of the Buddha) they sit for half-hour periods, the length of time it takes for a stick of incense to burn.

When wooden clappers are knocked together, they all get up walk round and round the room quite rapidly. This keeps the meditator awake. Then at a given signal, they

A great thing done is never perfect. But that does not mean it fails: it does exactly what it is. True wealth comes from having nothing. Because then you will never become drained.

go back to their cushions and meditate again.

Two monks stand at opposite ends of the room, each holding a long, flat stick shaped almost like a fan – thin at one end and rounded at the other. If one sees a monk slouching, sleeping, or goofing off in some way, he respectfully bows before the monk, who rests his head on his knees, and this fellow takes the stick and hits him vigorously on the shoulders. Most apologists for Zen say this is not punishment, it is simply to keep you awake. That is not true. I've investigated. It's the same as British boys' schools, only the Zen punishment doesn't have the same perverse qualities that British floggings do. Zen monks are cool about it, but the punishment is a fierce thing.

ABOVE If one sees a monk slouching, sleeping, or goofing off in some way... this fellow takes the stick and hits him vigorously on the shoulders.

BREATH COUNTING

At the beginning of *zazen* the monks do nothing but count their breathing. They count their breaths in tens, to allow their thoughts to still. Zen people do not close their eyes when they meditate, nor do they close their ears. They keep their eyes on the floor in front of them and they don't try to force away any sounds or other sensations.

This can become an extraordinarily pleasant occupation, listening to the little sounds of distant traffic, birds chirping, somebody banging a hammer, dogs barking or, especially, rain on the roof. The meditators don't block that out, but as time goes on, instead of counting breathing, they devote themselves to the koan that the *roshi* has assigned.

Every day the student goes to the teacher for *sanzen*, where he tries to present a satisfactory answer to the koan.

Sanzen is the moment in the monastery when no holds are barred, although the monks take a formal approach to it. The monk has to stop outside the master's quarters and knocks three times. At a signal from the master, he enters, sits down in the front of the master and bows down to the floor. Then the monk sits up, repeats the koan he has been given and offers his answer. If the master is not satisfied with the answer, he may simply ring his bell, which means: interview over, nothing doing. He may give the student a hint or puzzle him further.

The student is really being asked to be absolutely genuine. It is as if I said to you, 'Now, don't be self-conscious; I want you to be perfectly sincere. As a matter of fact, I am a mind-reader, and I know whether you are being sincere or not. I can see right down to that last little wiggly guzzle in the back of your mind.' If you think I can do that, then I'm putting you in a double-bind: I'm commanding you to be genuine. How can you possibly do that on command, especially when the person you are confronted with is a father figure, an authority figure?

SUPER-FATHERS OF SENSEI
In Japan, the *sensei* (teacher) is even more of an authoritative figure than one's father – which is saying a lot. You are being asked, in the presence of this tiger, to be completely spontaneous. As he rejects your answers again

and again, you get more and more desperate. The state called the 'great doubt' begins to build up. Soon the students are up to all kinds of tricks. They've read all the old Zen stories, and they come in with pieces of rock and wood, they try and hit the teacher, they do everything, anything – and yet it seems nothing will do.

I once knew an American who was given a particularly bothersome koan. One day he was going to the teacher for *sanzen* and saw a bullfrog sitting beside the path. (They have many bullfrogs in Japan, and they are all very tame.) He swooped up the frog and dropped it into the sleeve of his kimono. When he got to the master, the student produced the bullfrog. The master shook his head and said, 'Too intellectual.' Of course, the master meant not 'too intellectual' but 'too contrived', 'too premeditated'.

At that point, the students know they are just copying other people's Zen antics, something they just can't get away with. So they reach a state of total desperation. When the student reaches that point, the teacher starts encouraging him. He says, 'Come on, you're getting warm. But you must be ready to die for this.' Students have even vowed to commit suicide if they didn't get it in so many days. The time eventually comes when the

RIGHT In Japan, the *sensei* (teacher) is even more of an authoritarian figure than one's father... you are being asked, in the presence of this tiger, to be spontaneous.

Use up all you are, and then you can become new. Learn to have nothing and you will have it all. The Wise Ones always act like this, and are Children of the Tao. Never trying to impress, their being shines through.

When he sees that, the student has heard the sound of one hand or discovered who he was before his father and mother conceived him. Then the teacher says: 'Good. You have found the frontier gate to Zen. You've put your foot in the door, and you have crossed the threshold. But there is a long way to go: Now that you have found this priceless thing, you must double your efforts.' So the master gives the monk another koan.

GRADUATING IN ZEN

This course of training may take a long time. Eventually, though, the day of graduation comes, and there is a great hullabaloo, and everyone comes to salute the departing monk as he leaves to become a layman, a temple priest or even a *roshi*.

Zen is dangerous, too. People could easily go crazy under this sort of strain without a good adviser. It is also clear that this method of Zen training is unsuited to the modern age – witnessed by the fact that the temples are relatively empty. Hosen-ji, the biggest temple in Kyoto, is built to house six hundred monks, but today there are only eighty. You might think that is quite a crowd, but it isn't many compared to the old days.

To young people in Japan today, the Zen monastic life is quite incomprehensible; most see no point in it, save a few sons of the clergy carrying out the family tradition. Japanese Zen tradition, as in all these ancient organizations,

student can go in front of the master and not give a damn because he sees; he's seen the point. There was never a problem in the first place – he made up the problem himself. He then projected it on this master, who simply made the monk feel more stupid.

The student will go on struggling until he sees the foolishness of thinking he is separate from life and that he can get the better of it. This illusion of beating the game, of finding the thing out, dissipates.

Working on a koan is like a mosquito biting an iron bull. It is the nature of the mosquito to bite; it is the nature of an iron bull to be unbitten. The struggle with the koan is an exaggerated form of what everybody is ordinarily trying to do – to beat the game.

ABOVE The teacher says, 'You have found the frontier gate to Zen. You've put your foot in the door, and you've crossed the threshold. But there is a long way to go.'

is old and set in its ways. Since the time of Hakuin (1689–1768) the koans have been given fixed answers – there is a prescribed way to answer, and the meditator must hit on it. After he has answered it, he has to find the poem from a little book called The Zenrin-kushu ('The Zen Forest Anthology'; *zenrin* means 'forest of Zen' or monastic community). Here the student locates the little couplet that represents the meaning of the koan.

There was a critical point in the seventeenth century when there were two very great masters, Hakuin and Bankei. The seventeenth century was tremendously important in Japanese history; it was a time of what we might call the 'democratization of culture'. Basho invented haiku poetry so that everyone could be a poet – not necessarily for publication but for fun. He invented the seventeen-syllable haiku as a result of his Zen feeling for nature so that everyone could compose it. Before that time, poetry had become so obscure, so effete and sophisticated, that only great literati could write it. Basho created the haiku based on the Zenrin-kushu poems, such as:

> That bird calls
>
> Mountain changes
>
> To be more mysterious

The first lines of which say;

> The wind drops
>
> But the flowers keep on falling
>
> The bird calls
>
> And the mountain becomes more mysterious

Haiku developed from that kind of short insight, that glimpse of nature. While Basho was taking poetry to the peasants, Bankei was taking Zen to them as well, to the farmers. His Zen ran on an entirely different system. He talked mainly about what he called *bussho*, the 'unborn', that which has not yet and never will arise. According to Bankei, in you is the unborn mind, given to you by your parents.

The mind begotten by and given to each of us by our parents is none other than the buddha-mind, birthless and immaculate, sufficient to manage all that life throws at us. A proof. Suppose at this very instant while you face me listening, a crow caws and a sparrow twitters somewhere behind you. Without any intention on your part to distinguish between these sounds, you hear each distinctly. In doing so you are hearing with the birthless mind that is yours for all eternity.

RIGHT Basho created the haiku based on the Zenrin-kushu poems, such as:

The wind drops

But the flowers

keep on falling...

Well, we are to be in this mind from now on, and our sect will be known as the 'buddha-mind' sect. To consider my example of a moment ago, once again if any of you feel you heard the crow and the sparrow intentionally, you are deluding yourselves for you are listening to me, not to what goes on behind you. In spite of this there are moments when you hear such sounds distinctly, when you hear with the buddha-mind of non-birth. Nobody here can deny this. All of you are living buddhas because the birthless mind, which each possesses, is the beginning and the basis of all.

Now if the buddha-mind is birthless, it is necessarily immortal, for how can what has never been born perish? You have all encountered the phrase 'birthless and imperishable' in the Sutras – not born, not dying – but hitherto you have not had the slightest proof of its truth. Indeed, I suppose like most people, you've memorized this phrase while being ignorant of the fact of birthlessness.

When I was twenty-five, I realized that non-birth is sufficient to all life, and since then, for forty years I have been proving it to people just like you. I was the first to preach this greatest truth of life. I ask, have any

of you priests heard anybody else teach this truth
before me? Of course not.

A priest said to him, 'Once in the buddha-mind, I
am absentminded.' Bankei says, 'Well, suppose you are
absentminded as you say. If someone pricks you in the
back would you feel the pain?' 'Naturally.' 'Then you are
not absent-minded. Feeling the pain, your mind would
show itself to be alert.'

A layman says, 'Though I undertake Zen discipline,
I often find myself lazy, weary of the whole thing,
unable to advance.' And he replies, 'Once in the buddha-
mind there is no need to advance, nor is it possible to
recede. Once in birthlessness, to attempt to advance is

to have receded from the state of non-birth. A man
secure in that state need not bother himself with
such things, he's above them.'

The buddha-mind in each of you is immaculate.
All you've done is reflected in it. But if you bother
about one such reflection, you are certain to go astray.
Your thoughts don't lie deep
enough, they arise from the
shallows of your mind.

Remember that all you see
and hear is reflected in the
buddha-mind and influenced by
what was previously seen and

FOLLOWING SPREAD

...The bird calls, And the
mountain becomes more mysterious.
Haiku developed from that
kind of short insight,
that glimpse of nature.

The greatest straightness seems bent, the greatest skill seems awkward, the greatest speech, like a stammering. Act calmly, not coldly. Peace is greater than anger. Tranquillity and harmony are the true order of things.

heard. Needless to say, thoughts aren't entities. So if you permit them to rise, reflect themselves or cease altogether as they are prone to do, and if you don't worry about them, you will never go astray. In this way let a hundred, nay a thousand thoughts arise, and it is as if not one has arisen — you will remain undisturbed.

The only thing I tell my people is to stay in the buddha-mind. There are regulations, no formal disciplines. Nevertheless, they have agreed among themselves to sit in Zen for a period of two incense sticks daily — all right, let them. But they should well understand that the birthless buddha-mind has absolutely nothing to do with

LEFT *In this way, let a hundred, nay a thousand thoughts arise, and it is as if not one has arisen — you will remain undisturbed.* From Basho.

sitting with an incense stick burning in front of you. If one keeps in the buddha-mind without strain, there is no further satori *to seek.*

Whether awake or asleep one is a living buddha. Zazen means only one thing — sitting tranquilly in the buddha-mind. But really you know one's everyday life in its entirety should be thought of as a kind of sitting Zen. Even during one's formal sitting, one may leave one's seat to attend to something.

In my temple, at least, such things are allowed. Indeed, at some times it is advisable to walk in Zen for one incense stick's burning and sit in Zen for the other. A natural thing after all, one can't sleep all day, so one rises — one can't talk all day so one sits in Zen. There are no binding rules here.

FROM BASHO (MATSUO MUNFEFUSA)

Bankei was the *roshi* of Hosen-ji, and he stopped the use of the kaisaku stick to hit the monks when they were not meditating or were sleeping during meditation. He said, 'Even a sleeping man is still a buddha, and you shouldn't be disrespectful.'

He attempted a Zen of no methods: 'You can meditate if you want to. But that is like polishing a brick to make a mirror.' He used to say that trying to purify your mind was like trying to wash off blood with blood. But Bankei Zen was illusive. Hakuin had eight successors, while Bankei had none, and to some that was the most admirable thing about him.

*Only when you have nothing in your mind and no mind in things
are you vacant and spiritual, empty and marvellous.*

7

THE GATELESS GATE

NOTHING TO SAY

To the average person, who may not be well acquainted with the great books of Asia, The Gateless Gate is a book of extraordinary difficulty, despite the fact that it is written very simply. The title of this book is the Mumonkan (in Chinese, Wu-men-kuan), which is literally translated as 'no gate barrier'. So you might call it 'The Gateless Gate' or 'The Gate Which is No Gate'. This book is representational of the Zen school, or Chan in Chinese. The Zen school of Buddhism has been one of the most potent influences in the history of Far Eastern culture and has played an important role in the shaping of a wide range of its arts, from painting and calligraphy at one extreme, to jujitsu at the other. The influence of Zen can also be seen in landscape architecture, domestic architecture, ceramics, archery, fencing, all kinds of culinary arts and daily life itself. Because Zen has been such a formative influence in China and Japan, it is one of the most important systems of Asian philosophy for us to understand.

Zen is an extraordinary phenomenon in the history of philosophy and religion, and the reason Zen is so peculiar is that it has no doctrines that can be stated in words and nothing that it requires anybody to believe. In fact, it does not have anything to say at all. Zen is

See the wonder, the root of all.
Even if you cannot grasp its
nothingness, you can still see
something of the Tao in everything.
All mysteries are Tao, and
Heaven is their mother.
She is the gateway.

remarkable because it endeavours to convey its message – the realization that constitutes awakening – through experience and without the intermediary of words and ideas.

There is one technique I would like to concentrate on because it helps to sum up the character of Zen Buddhism, and that is direct pointing, a method in which Zen excels. Zen understands that human beings are seeking all that they fundamentally desire – be it complete contentment of the heart or an understanding of why this universe exists and what our place in it is – and this is not something obscure and far off, but something completely obvious. It is lying open for us to look at it in the immediate moment in which we are living. Zen all but says that the whole secret of life,

LEFT The Zen school has been one of the most potent influences in the history of Far Eastern culture… The influence can also be seen in the landscape architecture.

everything you could possibly desire, is yours at this moment. And if you cannot lay hold of it now, you will never be able to.

It is hard to convince people of this by talking or writing about it, because all talk and all systems of ideas (written or otherwise) are, in relation to reality itself, somewhat like a menu in relation to dinner. Those who try to get wisdom out of books or find comfort by believing in various systems of ideas and philosophies are really devouring the menu instead of eating the dinner. How, then, does one divert one's attention from the menu to the dinner itself? There is only one way: stop talking about it, stop writing about it and point directly at it. This is what Zen does, and most of the stories from the Mumonkan are examples of direct pointing.

BODHIDHARMA AND EKA

The first story I am going to read from the Mumonkan (which was compiled by a Zen master who lived in China between 1183 and 1260 CE), is the story of the encounter between Bodhidharma and his first disciple, Eka (in Chinese, Hui-k'o). Bodhidharma sat facing a wall. His future successor, Eka, stood outside in the snow.

I should first explain that Bodhidharma had emphatically discouraged Eka from becoming his disciple. This is always the way with Far Eastern philosophical and spiritual teachers: they do not look for disciples. The reason Bodhidharma was not looking for disciples was his own fundamental feeling that he had nothing to teach. The truth of Buddhism was so obvious that anyone could see it if they looked. To talk about it and try to teach it was, as they say in Zen, only to put legs on a snake. A snake moves very well without legs, and if you stick some on him it would only embarrass him.

So Bodhidharma had repeatedly said to Eka: 'I have nothing to teach. Go away!' But Eka was convinced that Bodhidharma had some secret that he could convey. So at last, as a token of sincerity, the student cut off one of his arms, while standing outside the teacher's hut in the freezing snow. As he presented the arm to his teacher, he said, 'My mind is not pacified. Master, pacify my mind.'

And Bodhidharma said, 'If you bring me that mind, I will pacify it for you.'

Eka replied, 'When I search for my mind, I cannot hold on to it.'

Bodhidharma told him, 'Then your mind is pacified already.'

It is said that at this moment Eka had a sudden insight into the whole mystery of life, the problem of peace of mind and the essential meaning of Buddhism itself.

To each one of these stories, the editor of The Gateless Gate has added a comment and a poem. First I give you the comment, then the poem.

That broken-toothed old Hindu

Bodhidharma came thousands of miles over the sea from India to China as if he had something wonderful. He is raising waves without wind. After he remained for years in China, he had only one disciple, and that one lost his arm and was deformed. Alas, ever since, he has had brainless disciples.

And the poem:

Why did Bodhidharma come to China?

For years monks have discussed this.

All the troubles that have followed since came from that teacher and disciple.

It is a characteristic convention of Zen literature that the masters of this school poke fun at one another, because insofar as they

PREVIOUS SPREAD

Bodhidharma was not

looking for disciples… The

truth of Buddhism was so

obvious that anyone could

see it if they looked.

seem to be masters, they realize that calling themselves 'masters' is kind of a joke. A master is, after all, one who has something to teach. And in Zen there is nothing to teach. The more one tries to explain Zen, the more obscure it becomes – just like the more one explains the joke, the less funny it seems. Going back to the story about Bodhidharma and Eka, Eka is expressing a very ordinary human problem. He says, 'I have no peace of mind.' What does he mean by 'mind'? We might say 'soul', we might say 'ego' or 'self'. 'I feel that I am unhappy, I need peace,' Eka says. And so Bodhidharma replies, very naturally, 'Bring out this soul, this mind of yours, and I will pacify it.' But Eka says, 'When I try to find myself, I cannot. I look and look, but then I realize that I am looking for the one who is looking, and I can never lay hold of it.'

Bodhidharma tells him, 'There, your mind is pacified already.'

FINDING OURSELVES

I feel diffident, really, about making any comment on a story of that kind. But in the nature of a hint, I will say that we are all convinced that we exist as a kind of self or ego, and our 'self-ishness' is one of our major problems.

It would be fascinating to discover that

Can you empty your mind of all dross, without throwing out the Tao? Can you do it without self-interest, so that you shine like a diamond? Can you turn yourself around and let the Tao rise up over you?

when we looked for ourselves, we were not really there, wouldn't it? And where we expected to find ourselves, in the centre of all our experience, we found only a hole, an empty space. The problem of our selves, our happiness, our peace of mind, would have just disappeared. There would be no 'one' whom one had to pacify or please; one was simply not there.

Of course, you cannot discover that just by hearing about it. You have to look and see. 'Who are you?' is one of the fundamental questions in all Eastern philosophy. Trying to find out 'who' is trying to find out who it is that is trying to find out. This is, after all, a parable of what we in the West call 'self-seeking.' It is as futile as somebody sitting down solemnly in a chair and gnashing and gnashing away, trying to bite their own teeth.

REALITY: THE BUDDHA

Another story from the Mumonkan is about a teacher called Tung-shan (Tosan). One day, when he was weaving some flax, a student came to him and asked, 'What is buddha?' (This question can mean, 'What is reality?' or 'What is it to be awakened?')

Tung-shan answered, 'This flax weighs three pounds.'

Now I will read you the comment:

With Tung-shan, Zen is like a clam. The minute the shell opens you see the whole inside.

And then the poem:

Three pounds of flax in front of your nose.
Close enough and the mind is still closer.
Whoever talks about affirmation and
    negation lives in the right and wrong region.

You must not suppose that there is some symbolism in saying 'This flax weighs three pounds'. Commentators have tried to explain that in Buddhism there are three

BELOW 'What is reality?' or 'What is it to be awakened?' … with Tung-shan, Zen is like a clam. The minute the shell opens you see the whole inside.

precious jewels: the Buddha himself; the *dharma*, his doctrine; and the *sangha*, his ordained followers. But the three pounds of flax do not refer to the three jewels. Tung-shan answered, 'This flax weighs three pounds,' just as you might answer a very simple question like, 'Where are you going?' And you reply, 'Well, I am going to town to buy groceries.' Or, if asked, 'What kind of a day was it yesterday where you live?' you say, 'It was raining a good deal of the time.' 'This flax weighs three pounds,' is an answer precisely like that. But it seems a strange answer to give to a question like, 'What is reality?'

Zen teaches that this tradition of answering questions in a simple and direct way derives from the Buddha himself.

MAHAKASHYAPA

Once, when the Buddha was lecturing in the mountains, he held a flower before his listeners and turned the flower in his fingers. Everyone was silent. Only Mahakashyapa smiled at this revelation, although he tried to control the lines of his face. The Buddha said: 'I have the eye of the true teaching. The heart of nirvana, of awakening, the true aspect of the formless, and the ineffable stride of the doctrine – it is not expressed by words but is transmitted beyond teaching. This teaching I

LEFT Tung-shan answered, 'This flax weighs three pounds'… it seems a strange answer to give to a question like, 'What is reality?'

The Tao pours out everything into life. It is a cornucopia that never runs dry. It is the deep source of everything. It is nothing, yet in everything. It smooths round sharpness and untangles the knots.

now give to Mahakashyapa.' And now the amusing commentary of the Mumonkan:

The golden-faced Buddha thought he could cheat anyone. He made the goodlessness as bad, and sold dog meat under the sign of mutton. And he himself thought it was wonderful. What if the audience had all laughed together? How could he have transmitted the teaching?

If Mahakashyapa had not smiled, how could he have transmitted the teaching? If Buddha had said that realization could be transmitted, then he behaved like the city-slicker who cheats. And if he said it could not be transmitted, why did he approve of Mahakashyapa?

And then the poem:

At the turning of a flower, his disguise
  was exposed.
No one in heaven and earth can surpass
  Mahakashyapa's wrinkled face.

All those disciples were gathered around the Buddha expecting the usual daily words of wisdom. Instead, he said nothing. He just picked up a flower and held it in his hand. This is the same sort of answer Tung-shan gave when asked, 'What is reality?' and he said, 'This flax weighs three pounds.' An ordinary statement, just as holding up the flower is an ordinary action.

GUTEI'S FINGER

When Zen teachers began to answer questions about reality in this way, they had their imitators – those who thought they had to find a new religious fad and went around imitating these antics in order to seem wise and to collect followers. This is what happened to a person who tried that sort of thing.

Gutei (in Chinese, Chü-chih) raised his finger whenever he was asked a question about man. An attendant began to imitate him in this way. When anyone asked the boy what his master had preached, the boy would raise his finger. Gutei heard about the boy's mischief. He seized him and asked, 'What is the fundamental principle of Buddhism?' The boy raised his finger; at once Gutei cut it off. The boy cried out and tried to run away. But Gutei stopped him. When the boy turned his head to him, Gutei raised up his own finger. In that instant, the boy was enlightened.

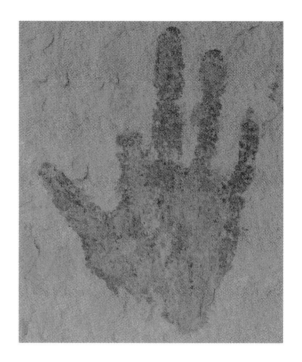

When Gutei was about to pass from this world, he gathered his monks around him. 'I attained my finger Zen from my teacher T'ien-lung [Tenryu]. And in my whole life I could not exhaust it.' Then he passed away.

So the secret of the thing is not just in being able to respond to questions with strange antics. The fellow who did not really understand but imitated his master's understanding got into very serious trouble. Yet despite getting into trouble, the fellow realized the thing in the end.

ABOVE The boy raised his finger; at once Gutei cut it off… When the boy turned his head, Gutei raised up his own finger. In that instant, the boy was enlightened.

It glows like the lamp that
draws the moth. Tao exists.
Tao is. But where it came
from, I do not know.
It has been shaping things
since before the First Being.
Before the Beginning of Time.

TIPPING OVER THE PITCHER

There is a Zen story that illustrates this point very well, and it is called 'The Story of Tipping Over the Pitcher'.

Yakujo wished to send a monk to open a new monastery. He told his pupils that whoever answered a question most ably would be appointed abbot. Placing a water pitcher on the ground, he asked, 'Who can say what this is without calling its name?' The chief monk said, 'No one can call it a wooden shoe.' But Isan, the cooking monk, tipped over the pitcher with his foot and went out. Yakujo smiled and said, 'The chief monk loses,' and Isan became the master of the new monastery.

The Mumonkan comments: Isan was brave enough, but he could not escape Yakujo's trick. After all, he gave up a light job and took a heavy one. Why can't you see he took off his comfortable hat and placed himself in iron stocks?

If I talk all the time and never listen to what others have to say, I lose touch with my fellow man. In the same way, if I think all the time – which is talking to myself, in a way – I lose touch with the reality that words are intended to symbolize. Zen's fundamental insight is that by an excess of thinking, men have lost touch with the real world. The solution to this problem is to be silent in one's mind and to look again at the real world, not thinking, but seeing it directly. This can't be talked about. If I want you to listen to music, any counsel to do so will drown out the music. The most direct way is for me to play the music itself.

The monk had seen that the reality of the pitcher was not the word or the idea 'pitcher', but something nonverbal. By kicking it over, he demonstrated his understanding.

This is, indeed, a central point of Zen, of Buddhist understanding in general: reality is beyond words. One must not confuse the world of things – as we think about, talk about and name them – with the world as it actually is. The first story I told was a case in point, because in the world of words, conceptions and inherited social notions, every one of us is convinced that he is a 'self'. But when we step out of that world into the clear daylight of reality with wide-open eyes, looking for ourselves – what do we find?

The Wise do not need to travel. They know there is nowhere to go.
They see without needing to look. They act by just being.

8

ZEN AND THE ARTS

WE ARE GOING to spend some time on Zen and the arts, but first, I want to give you a theoretical outline of the whole situation as a preparation for the more concrete experiences that will follow. As I have been saying, Zen is, above all else, a way of concrete experience: it is not a theory. This is what puzzles Westerners so: you can't describe Zen, you can only show it. Because it is a way of living, a style of living, it is an experience of life that no theory can satisfactorily encompass. In this respect, Zen has the same basis as Buddhism and is, in fact, a form of Mahayana Buddhism, one of the two great divisions of the Buddhist world. The Mahayana path means the 'Buddhism of the Great Course', and this form of Buddhism is distributed all over northern Asia: Tibet, China, Mongolia and Japan. In contrast to this is Theravada Buddhism, the 'Way of the Elders', which is found in Ceylon [Sri Lanka], Burma [Myanmar], Cambodia, Thailand and southern Asia.

There is an important distinction between the two. Theravada Buddhism expresses a general attitude of weariness of the world and a desire to be relieved of physical experience. On the other hand, the Mahayana attitude expresses acceptance of the world and therefore contains within it a transforming principle. As a result of this attitude Mahayana Buddhism has had great creative energy. If you are weary of the world, the practice of art – that is to say, the incarnation of an inspiration in material form – does not really interest you. But if you feel that whatever the universe may be, it is still spiritual, you may want to anchor it and see it incarnated in terms of the earth and everyday life. In the same way, a radio requires not only an

antenna to receive the spiritual element but also a ground wire to connect the spiritual to the earthly. Zen has been supremely successful in relating the spiritual to the earthly, which is why it has been one of the most important factors in moulding the taste and direction of arts in the Far East.

When we ask, 'What is Buddhism?' one can answer in several ways. You can say that it is the *dharma*, meaning the method taught by Gautama Siddhartha, a young Hindu prince who lived shortly after 600 BCE: the method of meditation, of mind control, designed to bring about peace. To illustrate this, imagine yourself in a state where you are afraid of absolutely nothing, where life – the problems, the pressures and the pains of life or the threat of death – is something you have ceased to be concerned with. You have learned this attitude of absolutely not caring about anything – whether you starve, whether you suffer, whether you die – because everything is all an illusion. This is rooted in the Hindu attitude that the world we see around us is all vibration. What seems to be solid is only something vibrating faster than you, and so from the Hindu standpoint the whole thing is an enormous illusion.

You can see at the same time that there is a certain joyousness to this approach. You are not negating the world all the time, thinking that people shouldn't look beautiful or that food shouldn't taste good. And you could

Simplicity comes of letting go of what you want. If you've been true to yourself earlier in your life then te builds up in you like a well that never fails. Nothing is impossible, then — and nothing can stop you.

really cut loose with this attitude because, without fear, you could dance all kinds of fantastic dances, and if you were a cocky spirit you might challenge people to all kinds of contests in a test of nerves, knowing all along it was all an illusion. (Zen people do that, but in a very cool way. If you make too strong a challenge, though, or show too much 'courage', then they have doubts as to whether you really do see it or whether perhaps you are just pretending to see it and are overcompensating by coming on too strong.) Now that abandon, in a very simple way, is the basis of Buddhism.

The training of the type of people called buddhas ('awakened ones') or *bodhisattvas* ('awakened ones working in the world out of compassion for all sentient beings') is

ABOVE The Daruma doll is a legless doll, weighted at the bottom so that if it is knocked down it always rolls back into an upright position.

represented symbolically in Japan by a little toy called a 'Daruma doll'. Daruma is the Japanese way of pronouncing Bodhidharma. The Daruma doll is a legless doll, weighted at the bottom so that if it is knocked down it always rolls back into an upright position. A Zen person is said to depend on nothing, to be phased by nothing and therefore has no worries, anxieties or problems. He has no problems since he knows that the world is an illusion and that he himself is reality. The eternal energy of existence and life simply appears in all kinds of forms.

Of course, eternal reality is what is basic to you, and knowing that this eternal reality is utterly indestructible is the true basis for a lack of fear and anxiety. People come and people go, trees come and trees go, but they keep reappearing. Of course, when you see trees reappear, you say, 'Well, those are new ones. They're not the same ones as before.' The closer you look at any individual thing, the more different you find it from any other individual thing, but that is because you are looking closely. If you don't look closely, the leaves that came on the trees this year are just the same as last year's leaves. And if you don't look too closely at people, they are always the same – droves and droves of them doing the same things, having the same problems, living out the same patterns. One after another they keep on coming. But when you start looking closely, you notice the differences and you say

'Aha! Look, it's an individual, like me.'

If you take in only the close view you lose sight of the forest for the trees. You don't realize what the wide vision gives you. Zen teaches a combination of close and wide vision, both at once. The whole nature of Buddhism is to deliver human beings from anxiety and panic about being alive.

The words 'anxiety', 'worry', 'panic' and 'terror' are all summed up in the Sanskrit word *duhkha*, which we usually translate as 'suffering'. *Sukha* ('sweet') is actually the opposite of *duhkha*, so *duhkha* means 'sour', or a feeling that somehow life is sour. For example, take a look at the state of mind of a person who feels that the universe is a merciless trap in which 'I' have been caught. 'I was born into this without my own free will because my parents got me involved in it.

'So here I am: a hopeless, helpless victim of circumstances.' That is *duhkha*. The Buddha realized that we are not the victim of circumstances at all. In his poem The Light of Asia Sir Edwin Arnold illustrates this:

You suffer from yourselves, none else compels,
None other holds you that ye live and die
And whirr upon the wheel, and hug and kiss
Its spokes of agony, its tire of tears, its nave of nothingness.

It's all up to you. You blame circumstances, people, society and parents only to the degree that you experience yourself as something separate. But if you clarify your consciousness and clarify your sense organs, you will see that the world and people around you are just as much 'you' as anything in your own body and brain. The whole thing is a unified, shifting organism or energy field, which comes on this way, that way, this way and that. Seeing this, you will begin to understand it in a multitude of ways. But by having a myopic view because you are concentrating too much on a small area, you may forget this point or fail to sense it to begin with.

In Buddhism this narrow, myopic view is called *avidya*, which literally means 'unknowing' or 'ignorance'. As a result of focusing too strongly on one area of life, you ignore the rest. You pick out one thing on which to concentrate, and the rest is disregarded. If you pick out the self inside this skin and say it is you, then you ignore the fact that you are also outside your skin. The real you is simply the cosmos, the energy that is filling all these vast spaces. There are galaxies, billions and billions of light years away, that are just as much you as the pupil of your eye. Distances have nothing to do with it because within the body, in scale, there are perfectly fabulous distances between your individual molecules, not to mention between atoms, electrons and so on. Space is relative: it is as big as you want to make it.

You can think about space and vast areas of the universe and say: 'How tiny we are, how unimportant.' But this is just one way of playing it. If you're feeling bad and you want to put yourself down, then that's the way you can think about it. On the other hand, if you are feeling up you can think about it quite differently. 'Good heavens, you mean that my friends and relations, the astronomers, have all discovered the universe is that big? What fantastic brains these people have! See how big we are? How fantastic that such a small entity could contain in its consciousness such a vast cosmos.' Then you may feel very happy and remember to think that way when you want to bring yourself up. One can talk about all these things; the difficulty, though, is to have the nerve to be that way.

So Zen is a form of Mahayana Buddhism, which is a way of training people to release the anxiety of being an individual ego. Zen, however, is not purely Buddhistic. It combines Indian Buddhism and Mahayana Buddhism with Chinese Taoist philosophy and a certain amount of Confucianism. Taoism is the Chinese philosophy of nature. Tao means 'the Way' or 'the course of nature'. Taoism is a philosophy of relativity, which originally goes back beyond Lao-tzu, who wrote the Tao-te

The Wise One who walks the Way is like a river reaching the sea, gathering the waters of streams into himself as he goes.

ching and the I Ching (The Book of Changes). The I Ching is an analysis of the rhythms of energy based on the positive and the negative. All Chinese thinking deriving from the I Ching is based on the principle of co-relativity. The positive and negative aspects of energy – that is to say, vigour and tiredness, life and death, being there and being not there – these things mutually support each other. Just as in the Gestalt theory of perception you cannot see a figure without a background, you cannot experience a thing called energy, happening, life, vitality, unless there is a background called death in which nothing is happening. Likewise, the perception of an interval, a space, a 'nothing', is dependent in just the same way on the presence of a 'something'. In the second chapter of the Tao-te ching

RIGHT You can think about space and vast areas of the universe and say: 'How tiny we are, how unimportant.' But this is just one way of playing it.

PREVIOUS SPREAD

The positive and negative

aspects of energy –

vigour and tiredness, life

and death... these things

mutually support each other.

Lao-tzu writes:

When all the world knows
beauty to be beautiful,
There is already ugliness.
When all the world knows
goodness to be good,
There is already evil.

To be, and not to be, arise mutually. Long and short are mutually distinguishable. High and low are mutually positive. That is why Lao-tzu writes (in the preceding chapter):

That the Tao, the course of nature
Cannot be put into words
Any Tao that can be described
Is not the eternal Tao

You cannot put into words what black and white have in common. You have to think about black as black, white as white. Certainly what they have in common isn't grey. Since all the words and ideas that we have are class words – labels on intellectual boxes – it is impossible to conceptualize what opposing experiences have in common. But if you attend to what is in common between life and death, between pleasure and pain, even if you cannot explain it, you don't have any problems. Attaining enlightenment cannot be an idea – it has to be something that is beyond ideas, an experience. Of course, intellectually, there can be no such experience, because when you talk about experience you sort it into the classes of logic and language. This is why Zen is described as a direct transmission of the

Understand the thrust of the
yang. But be more like yin
in your being. Be like a valley
that parts to its stream.
Be like a stream for the Earth...
and channel it so that it
flows – to the sea.

Buddha's experience outside the scriptures and the traditions. Zen does not depend on words and letters, but points directly to your self and attaining buddha-hood, awakening.

Zen, therefore, is a compound of Indian Buddhism, Taoism and, finally, Confucianism, which is an odd element in the whole picture. There is something very important to the nature of Zen that we have reason to see, and Confucianism seems to be quite the opposite of all this. Confucianism is the ritualistic order of Chinese social life and is very concerned with good manners, ceremoniousness, family order, obedience to parents, proper decorum and comportment. In Chinese history there is a playful battle between the Taoists and the Confucians, and the Taoists are always laughing at the Confucians.

One example of this ideological split between Confucians and Taoists is illustrated in an early Confucian concern, what they would call the 'rectification of names' – and that is being quite sure that the dictionary is in proper order. The dictionary is a terribly important book for a civilization, because if we don't have a clear idea of what we mean by our words we live in confusion. The Confucians were literati, greatly occupied with books, classics and the definition of words. By contrast, the Taoists were concerned with nature, with the actual experience of water and vegetables and birds. Their writings were full of descriptions, but the Confucians never looked outside the books. These schools correspond roughly to the differentiation in medieval Europe between scholastics and naturalists. The scholastics looked to the Bible for everything, and if it wasn't explained there, it wasn't true because all knowledge was taken from the book. The naturalists experimented with nature, and the mystics went along with the naturalists, which is why the Church didn't take kindly to the mystics, because they were having experimental knowledge of God instead of knowledge of God based on the authority of the texts. The Confucians are quite similar to the Western scholastics, except the Confucian way of life is not a religion and therefore does not necessarily exclude the domain of spiritual experience or mysticism.

Confucianism is a social ritual, and it is in this sense human-hearted.

YANG AND YIN

Man is understood by the Confucians as being a blend of the *yang* and the *yin*, in pretty much the same way that the Taoists understand those terms. We are part good, co-operative and rational; and part passionate, selfish and wayward. Confucianism believes that both these aspects of man must be recognized and played against each other, without animosity, in a co-operative way. The Confucian ideal of justice is compromise. Instead of determining whether you are clearly right or wrong, a decision in justice is based on the idea that both

BELOW Man is… a blend of the *yang* and the *yin*… We are part good, co-operative and rational; and part passionate, selfish and wayward.

are human qualities. Therefore, if you are reasonable people, you will come to a settlement out of court. Equity, rather than law, is the guiding principle of Confucian ideas of social order.

But along with this, Confucians emphasize the importance of reverence in everything you do, almost like Albert Schweitzer's reverence for life, except the Confucians express their reverence to everything. Think (in this context) of any suburban cook-out in the United States, where the father presides over the barbecue. There is something special about it. He may put on an apron or a chef's hat and may stand at the barbecue with great concentration on those steaks. At that moment he is a kind of king, a priest of the household; he is very careful and has everything just right for the ritual of cooking. In that moment, he is experiencing what the Confucians call 'the reverence attitude'. According to their ideas, everything you do should be done that way. The Confucian ideal is that life should be carried out with the utmost regard for all material things, possessions and people. Everything is ceremonious.

Everything done in a Zen monastery is also done with this reverence. But there is a very funny difference — which I have had a great deal of difficulty identifying — between the reverence attitude in Zen (and in the Far East in general) and the idea of reverence in Christianity. The Zen people, as you can see in many drawings, make extremely irreverent caricatures of the patriarchs of Buddhism. They make them look like bums. At the same time, you will see these gorgeous rituals conducted in Zen monasteries where everybody is bowing. They even prostrate themselves on the floor in front of an image of the Buddha. I have tried in the monasteries to look into these people's faces, but sometimes you see an absolutely impenetrable mask of equanimity. At other times there is a certain look in their eyes; it indicates that in this reverence there is a certain twinkle, a certain challenge. The Zen recitation of sutras is different from the chanting of the Psalms or hymn-singing. The Hindu chants, as well, display no terror of the cosmos; rather, they express a joining with whatever it is that goes on. It isn't a guilt-based worship, but it is at the same time respectful.

Japanese people always bow to each other — they bow interminably. This is not quite a gesture of subservience, though it reflects this Confucian attitude. The Zen monks brought Confucianism into Japan, and they established Confucian ideas as the basis of Japanese views on the social order, propriety and how things should be carried along. From our point of view today, we would say that most Confucian ideas are pretty stuffy, but they did embody a

subtle respect. I have heard a story told of an American tourist businessman who once went to Tibet. He was shown into a monastery, and in the great sanctuary a light was burning. Two lamas were standing in their meditation inside this light, and the monks explained that the light had been burning for a thousand years. The American looked at it and blew it out.

Sometimes, of course, this reverence can be extreme, even silly. There is a story of an old master who was travelling along a mountain road to visit a Zen monastery. He came upon a small stream and noticed a lettuce leaf floating down it; he shook his head and thought, 'That's a very bad monastery up there if they let a lettuce leaf go down the stream – so wasteful!' Suddenly, through the bushes there came crashing an enormous monk, who

What is built on rock can never be pulled down. What is held lightly can never be lost. Meditate on the virtue within yourself, and your virtue will last for generations.

swooped down and retrieved the leaf from the water. 'Oh,' the old master said, 'It's OK after all.' The energy that the monk would have gained from eating the lettuce leaf was far less than the energy he expended to chase it. He wasn't very economical, but still, that's the sort of attitude you find in Zen – nothing is to be wasted. Every now and then, when you eat in Japan (especially in a Zen monastery), you must be careful to take up every grain of rice in your bowl – leave nothing. This is all part of the Confucian respect for the material environment and for every piece of clothing, tool, structure, animal or person.

LEFT When you eat in Japan (especially in a Zen monastery), you must be careful to take up every grain of rice in your bowl – leave nothing.

SUICIDAL ZEN

Conversely, there is also another strong attitude in Zen: 'Nothing is good which cannot be destroyed.' If the situation isn't right, Zen people may demolish it all. In other words, at the right moment, blot it all out and start again.

Buddhism came to China as a more or less monastic form of life, because this understanding was cultivated in the Indian tradition of monastic communities – communities for men and communities for women. In order to become free of hang-ups, the adepts did not want to bother about spouses and children, all of which had to go. The Chinese didn't take to that premise very kindly; in China the family was absolutely fundamental. The Chinese began to make compromises. Instead of teaching the ideal of the monk who completely abandoned the world forever, they developed the idea of the monastery as a training school into which young men and women went. After completing their training, the monks and nuns could go back into everyday life. A few remained as teachers, and some of these became the great masters. So in the great golden age of Chinese culture, there was a terrific flowering of Chinese culture, art and philosophy. This was the period when the first European travellers visited China and were so astounded with its greatness in comparison to what they knew. The Zen way of life was a primary foundation

and towards the material and natural world rather than the human. Zen people in China or Japan did not initiate any distinguished social service projects. Most of the influence of Zen was, to our befuddlement, on art and war. Part of the reason for this is that the agrarian cultures of Asia regarded the human situation as insoluble. They didn't think anything could be done about it. They didn't have the technological ability to solve the problem of poverty, and, therefore, they took the dog-eat-dog situation among human beings as a foregone conclusion. Nothing could be done to ameliorate it, except to stop caring or stop being frightened of it. So Zen expressed itself primarily in craft, art, pottery, architecture, sculpture, painting, gardening, calligraphy, military athletics and poetry.

However, Zen isn't a curious Oriental cult. Everybody has Zen in some way, because everyone does something perfectly. You might say that even the stupidest human being could grow beautiful hair or have lovely eyes. And that is the person's Zen – what they do without calculation, without affectation – which is natural, spontaneous, gorgeous. Now a great artist tries to do whatever his art is – be it dancing or painting or fencing – in the same way as they turn their eyes blue. There is no awkwardness in it connected to self-consciousness. All awkwardness in art is a kind of hesitation, and this is called in Zen 'an evil passion' or 'defilement'. In the performance of

ABOVE Zen people... did not initiate any distinguished social service projects. Most of the influence of Zen was, to our befuddlement, on art and war.

of this flowering.

Zen migrated to Japan in approximately 1200 CE, where it exerted a similarly vigorous effect on the subsequent development of Japanese culture. It puzzles Westerners that the expression of Zen is oriented towards art rather than technology, any art, the artist must get rid of their hesitation.

This, then, is what happens in the course of Zen training. Here is an individual who is not overly aware of his behaviour but is actually something of a mess. Life will always eventually challenge such a person in some way, making him nonplussed. So he seeks out the wise man, and says, 'I'm in trouble.' In the training process, which Zen is, the master does everything possible to nonplus the student – to catch him off guard, make him self-conscious and throw him off track. The master has many ways of doing this; his method is to catch the false mode in other people. If there is some little thing that shows that all this gamesmanship is self-protection from the

That which is iron hard is dead, and that which is fluid and sensuous and rippling is alive. That is why a huge army, with all its strength and complacency, will be defeated — like a great tree axed down.

fundamental fear, the Zen master figures it out and throws it right back at the students. The students just know what to do with it.

This doesn't occur only in everyday personal relations but also in tiny things, such as how one lifts a spoon; it's possible to make someone completely awkward about that, too. The masters go into endless conniptions about whether you lift your spoon in the right way, but it is all intended, not to teach you the ritual of how to do it correctly, but to use the ritual to see if they can faze you with it. If you are so anxious to do the ritual right that you can hardly hold on to that spoon, there is something wrong with you. So Zen is a process of constant testing to see whether a person is doing an action genuinely or whether they are a phoney.

LISTENING TO ZEN

Zen is always visible, and it's much easier to see through looking than to hear through words, although you can hear Zen if you listen to the sound of the words rather than what they are supposed to mean. You may have heard in passing of a kind of Buddhism known as the Shin sect or Jodo-shin-shu, the 'Pure Land True Sect'. This is almost a sort of Buddhist Methodism because it belongs to the Tariki school, which teaches deliverance through the power of another, and is distinct from the Zen Jiriki school, which promulgates liberation through one's own effort.

There was once a member of the Tariki school who studied Zen. He was discussing with his teacher the idea behind the Tariki school, in which all you have to do to attain deliverance is to call on the name of the Buddha of Boundless Light. His name in Japan is Amida (in India, Amitabha). When you call on him in Japanese you recite the formula Namu Amida Butsu. Namu is the name of Amida Butsu, the Buddha Amida. So this is called nembutsu (from nem, 'thought' or 'recollecting'): thinking about Buddha. All you have to do in this school, therefore, is say Namu Amida Butsu once and you will be born in the Pure Land presided over by the Buddha Amida. Becoming a buddha is a cinch.

Getting enlightened by this method is easy, because in this world everybody is trapped in vicious circles, creating so much bad karma that there's no way out. According to this doctrine, all good actions and practices of meditation for deliverance make the situation even worse because they merely build up one's spiritual pride.

In Zen you cannot attain enlightenment by effort. There is a poem that says:

You cannot get it by grasping
You cannot get it by not grasping
Or you cannot get it by thinking
You cannot get it by not thinking.

So how are you to get enlightenment? You have to find out there's no way to get it. And this is what the nembutsu technique also does. So when a Tariki priest was studying Zen with his master, he wrote a poem to try to express his understanding. The poem was:

When the nembutsu is said
There is neither Buddha nor oneself;
Namu Amida Butsu
Only the sound is heard.

But the Zen teacher didn't quite like that. So he corrected the poem to read:

When the nembutsu is said
There is neither Buddha nor oneself;
Namu Amida Butsu
Namu Amida Butsu.

The priest had added one line too many. But you see, you can get it through sound, and you can get it through sight. But as long as we talk about it we will never get it, because we don't really hear the sound. We don't get beyond the world of concepts and ideas – although you also need to be careful here. When the master Joshu was asked, 'What do you say to someone who comes to you with nothing?' He answered, 'Throw it away.'

For this reason, Zen has expressed itself through the arts to an enormous degree. The tea ceremony in particular has been central to Zen because it is like opera in the sense that opera involves many arts – music, drama, staging, ballet and so on. The people who developed the tea ceremony became masters of

PREVIOUS SPREAD The
people who developed the
tea ceremony became masters
of aesthetics, because every
one of the arts... collects
around the ceremonial.

aesthetics, because every single one of the arts — ceramics, bronze-making, painting, architecture, gardening, the cultivation of rocks — collects around the ceremonial.

To explain this I must tell you something of its history.

THE TEA CEREMONY

There is a legend that explains the history of tea. Bodhidharma fell asleep during meditation one night. When he woke up, he was so furious at himself for having gone to sleep that he cut off his eyelids and threw them on the ground. Immediately the first tea plant grew; the leaves of the tea plant were shaped like eyelids. Thereafter, everybody who wanted to stay awake drank tea.

All religions have a characteristic drink.

Can you nurture your souls by holding them in unity with the One. Can you focus your ch'i — your energy — and become as supple, as yielding as a baby?

Christianity has wine, which it shares with Judaism; both use wine as sacrament. For Islam the characteristic drink is coffee; for Hinduism, milk; for Buddhism, tea. There is a saying that 'the taste of Zen and the taste of tea are the same'. This is actually a pun, because in Chinese Zen is Chan, and tea is cha. 'Tea taste' means in both the Japanese and Chinese worlds not only the actual taste of tea on the tongue but the taste that goes with tea, the taste of tea masters. Zen monks from the earliest times drank tea to be in a state of wakefulness. Tea is a mild psychedelic, especially in the form the monks drink it — not the ordinary steeped tea leaves but very finely powdered tea, which can be mixed at great strength with powerful results. The monks found it good for achieving total clarity of mind. So those monks, meditating without shutting out their senses but only quieting their thoughts, came to a strange understanding of the incredible beauty of ordinary things — the sound of wind, the taste of water and the appearance of the simplest utensils used in everyday life.

When the mind reaches a certain kind of clarity and serenity, all those ordinary things become apparent, and you are living in an enchanted world. So the true spirit of the tea ceremony is one of very great simplicity — enjoying the 'just so-ness' (in Japanese, *konomama*) of what is just so. This ceremonial doesn't look religious, it looks ritualistic,

because it works with respect for ordinary things. There is no god being worshipped, but there is a realization that ordinary, everyday life is divine.

One of the great creators of the tea ceremony was a man named Sen-no-rikyu. Many of the tea masters of today are in some way descended from him, and they all have the family name Sen. Sen-no-rikyu was a Zen student, and he had an aesthetic that influenced everything used in the ceremony. For example, the traditional bowl is not the sort of thing you associate with fine Chinese porcelain – eggshell china with plum blossom designs. The tea ceremony bowls are made of the roughest clay used by poor peasants. As a result of the tea cult and of Sen-no-rikyu, some examples of these bowls a few hundred years old are displayed in museums and are worth thousands of dollars. However, modern tea bowls are still made in the tradition of the ancient bowl makers, and as many people practice the cult of tea in Japan, they are very inexpensive. And this spirit has also influenced American pottery, because this spirit – the splendour of the extremely primitive and simple – encourages a clear mind.

ABOVE The tea ceremony bowls are made of the roughest clay used by poor peasants… some examples are worth thousands of dollars.

You cannot describe it, you cannot admire it, you cannot feel it.
It is your real self, which has no hiding place.

9

RETURN TO THE FOREST

THE SYMBOL WITHOUT MEANING

During the past few months, I have been studying an extraordinary paper written by Joseph Campbell, familiar to many of you as the author of a book on mythology called The Hero with a Thousand Faces. The paper I mention was presented in 1957 at a conference in Switzerland. A meeting of scholars, philosophers, psychologists and scientists gathers every year under the auspices of a woman who has long been interested in the work of C.G. Jung. Campbell's paper was called 'The Symbol Without Meaning'.

It explores an extraordinary phenomenon in the history of religions; you might call this phenomenon 'into the beginning,' the development and disillusion of cosmologies of great views of the world, under religio-philosophical auspices, which are languages about the universe devised by various cultures.

Campbell distinguishes two great phases in religious history, equated with two styles of culture predating our own technological style: hunting cultures and agrarian cultures.

He points out that the kind of religious characteristic of a hunting culture is what we now call 'shamanism', although this particular word is distinctive of Mongolian primitive religion. Nevertheless, the phenomenon known as shamanism is found all over the planet. Shamanism is characterized by the fact that it is very individualistic. That is to say, the religious experience of the shaman is not something he gets from an authoritative priesthood. It is not something handed down from generation to generation or taught by human to human.

The shaman is a solitary medicine man, a man of power, who invariably has to find his experience for himself. Usually it means going alone into the dangers of the forest or jungle, or holing himself in his own hut for several days to undergo some kind of ordeal, not so much on the physical level as on the psychic level. The shaman goes through an adventure in the psychic world, the world of spirits. And when he comes through the other side of the ordeal, he emerges an initiate of power.

The individualistic character of this experience is important because it goes along with the style of a hunting culture, in which every individual contains the whole culture. Specialized functions, which contain a division of labour, are not needed in hunting cultures. The hunter spends much of his time on his own, and he must learn to take care of himself in the wild without any other human aid. Although there are societies and social groups in these cultures, they are centred around biological families – individuals and groups who are equals.

LEFT The shaman goes through an adventure in the psychic world, the world of spirits. And when he comes through the other side... he emerges an initiate of power.

An entirely different state of affairs arises in a settled, agrarian culture: because the style of life is more complex, a division of labour is required. Not only do you see a separation of humans into various castes and roles, but also development of more complex languages and institutions to provide communication between these castes.

This always involves a very, very powerful socialization of the individual, who spends more and more time in a settled place, where he has greater intercourse with other people. He has to learn to think in accordance with common patterns, based on things such as language, or type of work he is doing, or the geographical features of the area he inhabits.

Each individual has to subordinate himself to a socially implanted view of life, because only under these conditions is communication between individuals possible. And so the agrarian style, distinct from that of a hunting culture, is a traditional and authoritative religion, where the individual derives his experience from a tradition usually embodied in the priesthood.

Campbell also points out that the first historical appearances of the familiar circle symbol (in Sanskrit, the mandala) are associated with agrarian cultures. No example of this kind of symbol is found archeologically prior to the development of an agrarian community.

THE MANDALA

We might say something here about the mandala being a world mythological symbol, although anyone who has studied the words of C.G. Jung is familiar with it. A mandala is essentially a circle, usually divided into four quarters or multiples of four, and has in it the general theme of the integration of a community. It is not unlike a stockaded village, which has a ring of defence around a centre. Campbell shows that the symbol represents the formation of a society in which the human functions are divided. We find in many of these ancient societies that the primary social classes or functions are divided into four groups. For example, in medieval European society we have the spiritual power, the priesthood; the temporal power, the nobility; the commons; and the serfs.

In ancient Indian society, as well, we have the brahman caste, the priesthood; the kshatriya caste, the rulers and soldiers; the vaishya caste, the commons or merchants; and the shudra caste, the labourers. These four castes are represented by the four divisions of the mandala, the integrated, encircled community. Campbell emphasized that the community's religiousness was a common experience carried down by tradition — by an authority, the priestly caste. It had to be a

ABOVE A mandala is a circle,
usually divided into four
quarters, or multiples of
four, and has in it the
general theme of the
integration of a community.

common experience;
community life of this
kind depends on
communication. We can
communicate with each
other not only by sharing a
common language, but
more importantly, by sharing a common view
of the world and a common type of sensuous
experience. Those who have the type of
sensuous experiences that we call hallucinations
or visions do not fit easily into a community.

Campbell's paper shows that social
cosmologies – views of the world held in
common by societies – also tend to break up.

For example, the fifteenth-century expansion
of the Western world through exploration of
the globe and greater knowledge of astronomy
began to break up the geocentric view of the
Ptolemaic universe – the worldview under
which Christianity was born. Campbell looks
on this as a break-up of the mandala, the
dissolution of the communal, agreed, stable
picture of the world through which men were
able to communicate with each other. This
breaking-up, therefore, disrupts our means of
communication and throws the culture into a
state of fundamental confusion.

Perhaps it is because our unified worldview
is breaking up that we Westerners have become

interested in other cultures' attempts to deal with life as it must be lived, since we are confused by the relativistic world of modern thought.

The idea of moving beyond a communal view of the world and managing to get along without it is not new. In ancient Indian society – and to some extent, in modern India as well – when a man has done his work in the world and is able to hand over his caste duties (be they priestly, political, or professional) to his children, he abandons that world and becomes what is ordinarily called a *sannyasin*, a 'holy man', 'hermit' or 'spiritual devotee'.

The abandonment of caste is called entering into the state of *vanaprastha*. *Vanaprastha* in Sanskrit means 'a forest dweller'. In this sense, the man who gives up caste goes back to the way of life that predates the agrarian culture; he goes 'back' to shamanism. And this is true not only in Indian culture, but also in Chinese. The Confucian way of life also represents the community – the mandala – the enclosed, nice little world in which we feel we understand each other and our environment.

In China the Taoist philosophy corresponds to the Indian search for liberation (in Sanskrit, *moksha*) from the socially conditioned view of the world. Anthropological evidence shows a connection between the solitary Taoist sage and the shaman. And it is possible that the words shamana in Sanskrit and shaman in Chinese have their origins in the word 'shaman'.

Shamana refers to the sannyasin, the man who has given up social life in the world. Likewise the Chinese shaman is the lonely sage, questing for immortality, who has gone by himself into the mountains and the forests. Of course, we should not suppose that the entry into *vanaprastha*, or the Taoist sage's return to the forest, is (in the strict sense of the word) a regression. It's no more a regression than when we say that a wise man has become a child again.

We do not mean that he has literally become childish, that he has forgotten how to think, speak, and behave in human society. The person who enters in the stage of *vanaprastha* does not become a wolf-man, a sort of wild savage who runs around in the jungle naked and eats his food off the ground with his teeth. He does nothing of the kind. But there is some sort of analogy between 'going back to the shaman's religion' and 'going back to the life of the hunter', going beyond a society whose worldview is a conditioned social pattern.

In just what way is this going beyond society? How does it apply to our own situation, where we are not going voluntarily beyond a clear, authoritative, and comfortable view of the world? The very pressure of events forces us beyond this view by the uncertainty of our times and by the instability of modern thought, which offers us no secure, humanly comfortable picture of the universe.

TIME BINDING

First of all, one of the principal characteristics of a social system of communication is that communication is a form of what Alfred Korzybski has called 'time binding.' Thought and language involve a codification of experience, a way of thinking about life that is based on description.

Now, description is a way of coding, putting into symbols the events that go by us. As we learn to put events into symbols, we develop peculiar powers of memory. It becomes much easier to recollect and to formalize what has happened to us. Along with this naturally comes the ability to project our recollection into thoughts about the future course of events. Apparently, this is something that primitive human beings do but animals do not (to any extent).

But this ability to describe and to prefigure what is going to happen to us has a price: it has an alarming effect on our emotions. We are thereby able – in this ability to think about all sorts of possibilities – to experience the emotions that are appropriate to those possibilities and to turn them into present happenings.

Civilized man tends to be in a state of chronic fear and anxiety because he is always confronted, not with the simple actuality of what is happening before him, but with the

ABOVE When a man has done his work in the world… he abandons that world and becomes a *sannyasin*, a 'holy man', 'hermit' or 'spiritual devotee'.

innumerable possibilities of what might happen. And since his emotional existence is in a chronic state of anxiety and tension, he loses the ability to relate to the concrete world of the actual present. He becomes so tied up inside, the channels of his sensibility become blocked. He gets a kind of neurological sclerosis, an inability to give himself to spontaneity, to be alive with full joyous abandonment.

The more civilized we become, the more stuffy we get. Therefore the various ways of liberating ourselves from our society – of entering vanaprastha or going back to the forest – are increased, because more people reach a point in life when they say: 'Now look here, I have had enough of all this.'

The culturally embedded ability to go back to shamanism, to get away from the communal interpretation of how one ought to think and feel, arose in many great societies of the past. They rise again today.

It is perhaps impossible or misleading to have an authoritative attitude about this phase of human spiritual exploration. Sometimes, for example, when a person wants to find out who he really is, he goes to a psychiatrist. Occasionally he will find the kind of psychiatrist who does not have an authoritative view of human health and who simply helps the individual find his own way. Other times, unfortunately, he will find doctrinaire psychotherapists who think they know what an integrated, healthy, normal human being is, but

instead apply a speculative, theoretical pattern of human nature and the design of the psyche. These people may attempt, consciously or subconsciously, to wangle the patient into accepting this view. Alternatively, we may get from Asia accounts of their ways of liberation, which in many cases have hardened into orthodoxy.

ABOVE The culturally embedded ability to go back to shamanism… arose in many great societies in the past. They rise again today.

These accounts present their traditional spiritual experiences as if they were the kind of experiences that the priest imparts as his function. Thus, when we hear swamis represent an orthodox interpretation of moksha, or when we hear Zen masters articulate an orthodox Buddhist practice, we should be suspicious, because these are the kinds of

*Not knowing how near the
truth is, people seek it far
away — what a pity!
They are like him who,
in the midst of water,
cries in thirst so imploringly.*

experiences that cannot be transmitted.
By their very nature, these are experiences
one discovers for oneself. If they could be
explained, if they could be transmitted,
they would not be the very things that
they are intended to be.

It is in the nature of these experiences
of liberation that they cannot be codified or
incorporated into social communication. It
is fortunate that we in the West do not have
too many authoritative masters and teachers
to whom we can now go for enlightenment.

FOLLOWING SPREAD We are
going back, in a symbolic
sense, into the forest, like
the hunter of old, who has
nobody around him to tell
him how he ought to feel.

More and more of us
feel that we are all alone
together whistling in the
dark, that we do not have
a saviour. No statesman
is clever enough to
understand the frightful

tangle of international affairs or do much
about it. No psychologist or physician
or philosopher impresses us as having the
last word on everything. More and more,
each one of us is thrown on our
own resources.

What an excellent state of affairs! We
are going, in a symbolic sense, back into the
forest like the hunter of old, who has nobody
around him to tell him how he ought to feel
and how he ought to use his senses. Like
the hunter, we must therefore find out for
ourselves. When you study the records of
these self-discoveries, the fascinating thing
is that there seems to be a universal measure
of agreement among all those who have
already found out for themselves. Yet the
way they find out is not through seeking
agreement with others or trying to find
what others have found.

They always discover what their own senses
and their own direct experiences tell them
when they go into the 'inner closet' and ask for
a direct encounter with the world.

They are no longer looking out of the
corner of their eyes to see if everybody else is
doing the same thing or getting the same
results. It is in this exploration that a person
becomes in the truest sense of the word a
'self', an original, authoritative source of
life, as distinct from the person in its
original sense, a mask, a role that he is
playing in a society.

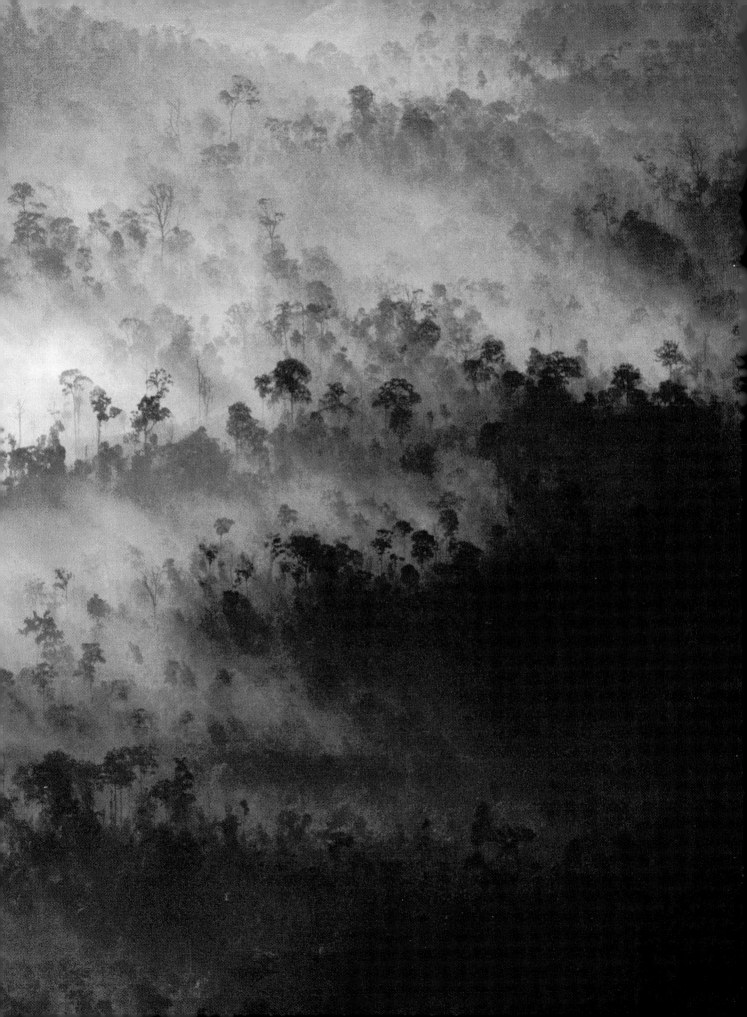

MORE INFORMATION

More information on Alan Watts is available through a special web site – alanwatts.com – that his son, Mark, set up after the philosopher's death. The web site includes a brief biography of Alan Watts and a list of his writings and recordings. The web site forms part of the Electronic University, which Mark began to continue his father's work, and to realize Alan Watts' vision of a way of education through electronic media. The following is a list of published works by Alan Watts. Some are now out of print but may still be available from many on-line book stores and specialist book shops.

OTHER WORKS BY ALAN WATTS

Become What You Are (ed. by Mark Watts), Shambala, San Francisco (USA), 1995

Behold the Spirit: A Study in the Necessity of Mystical Religion, Pantheon, New York (USA), 1947

Beyond Theology: The Art of Godmanship, Pantheon, New York, 1964

The Book: On the Taboo Against Knowing Who You Are, Pantheon, New York (USA), 1966

Buddhism: The Religion of No Religion (ed. by Mark Watts), Charles Tuttle, Boston (USA), 1996

Cloud-hidden, Whereabouts Unknown: A Mountain Journal, Pantheon, New York (USA), 1973; Abacus, Sphere, London (UK), 1977

Culture of Counter Culture (ed. by Mark Watts), Charles Tuttle, Boston (USA), 1998

Diamond Web: Live in the Moment (ed. by Mark Watts), And Books, South Bend (USA), 1987

The Early Writings of Alan Watts 1931-38 (ed. by John Snelling, Mark Watts and Dennis Sibley), Ten Speed Press, San Francisco, (USA), 1980; Thames & Hudson, London (UK), 1980

Erotic Spirituality: The Visions of Konarak, Collier Macmillan, New York (USA), 1971

In My Own Way (autobiography), Pantheon, New York (USA), 1972

The Essential Alan Watts (ed. by Mary Jane Watts), Celestial Arts, San Francisco (USA), 1974 (also published as *The Essence of Alan Watts*, 1976)

The Joyous Cosmology: Adventures in the Chemistry of Consciousness, Pantheon, New York, 1962

The Meaning of Happiness: The Quest for Freedom of the Spirit in Modern Psychology and the Wisdom of the East, Harper, New York (USA), 1940

The Modern Mystic: A New Collection of the Early Writings of Alan Watts, HarperCollins, New York (USA), 1989; Element, Shaftesbury, (UK), 1990 (also published as *Seeds of Genius*, Element, Boston (USA), 1996)

Nature, Man and Woman, Pantheon, New York (USA), 1958

Nonsense, Stolen Paper Editions, San Francisco (USA), 1967

Om: Creative Meditations (ed. by Mark Watts), Ten Speed Press/Celestial Arts, San Francisco (USA), 1979

FURTHER READING

Out of the Trap (ed. by Mark Watts), And
  Books, South Bend (US), 1985

The Philosophies of Asia (ed. by Mark Watts),
  Charles Tuttle, Boston, (USA) 1995

Play to Live (ed. by Mark Watts), And Books,
  South Bend (USA), 1982

*The Spirit of Zen: A Way of Life, Work and Art in the
  Far East*, Grove Press, New York (USA), 1936
  (revised 1958); John Murray, London
  (UK), 1936

Still the Mind: An Introduction to Meditation (ed. by
  Mark Watts and Marc Allen), Charles Tuttle,
  Boston (USA), 2001

Talking Zen (ed. by Mark Watts), Weatherhill,
  New York (USA), 1994

Tao: The Watercourse Way (ed. by Al Chung-liang
  Huang), Pantheon, New York (USA), 1975

Taoism: Way Beyond Seeking (ed. by Mark Watts),
  Charles Tuttle, Boston (USA), 1998

Tao: The Watercourse Way (ed. by Al Chung-liang
  Huang), Pantheon Books, New York
  (USA), 1975

The Tao of Philosophy (ed. by Mark Watts),
  Charles Tuttle, Boston (USA), 1995

*'This Is It' and Other Essays on Zen and Spiritual
  Experience*, Random House, New York
  (USA), 1958

The Two Hands of God: Myths of Polarity, Collier
  Macmillan, New York, 1963

*The Way of Liberation: Essays and
  Lectures on the Transformation of Self*
  (ed. by Mark Watts and Rebecca Shropshire),
  Weatherhill, New York
  (USA), 1983

The Way of Zen, Pantheon, New York (USA),
  1957; Penguin, Harmondsworth (UK), 1962

The Wisdom of Insecurity, Pantheon, New York
  (USA), 1951

Uncarved Block, Unbleached Silk: The Mystery of Life
  (ed. by Mark Watts), A&W, New York
  (USA), 1978

What is Tao?, New World Library,
  San Francisco, 2000

What is Zen?, New World Library,
  San Francisco (USA), 2000

ALAN WATTS MONOGRAPHS AND PAMPHLETS

An Outline of Zen Buddhism, 1932

Seven Symbols of Life, 1936

The Psychology of Acceptance, 1939

The Theological Mystica of St Dionysius, 1944

The Meaning of Priesthood, 1946

Zen Buddhism, 1947

Zen, 1948

The Way of Liberation in Zen Buddhism, 1955
Beat Zen, Square Zen and Zen, 1959

ALAN WATTS RECORDS

Om: The Sound of Hinduism, 1967

Why Not Now: Dhyana, The Art of Meditation, 1969

The Essential Lectures (each set of six CDs includes live lecture recordings; the series is also available in MP3 format)

The Tao of Philosophy: 'Slices of Wisdom', 'Images of God', 'Coincidence of Opposites', 'Seeing Through the Net', 'Myth of Myself', 'Man in Nature' and 'Limits of Language', Public Lectures, Electronic University, Mill Valley, San Francisco (USA), 1963-9

Philosophies of Asia: 'The Relevance of Oriental Philosophy', 'The Mythology of Hinduism', 'Eco-Zen', 'Swallowing a Ball of Hot Iron', 'Intellectual Yoga', 'Introduction to Buddhism' and 'Taoist Way of Karma', Public Lectures, Electronic University, Mill Valley, San Francisco (USA), 1968-71

Myth and Religion: 'Not What Should Be, But What Is!', 'Spiritual Authority', 'Jesus: His Religion?', 'Democracy in Heaven', 'Image of Man' and 'Sex in the Church', Public Lectures, Electronic University, Mill Valley, San Francisco, 1966-72

Buddhism: Religion of No Religion: 'The Journey from India', 'The Middle Way', 'Buddhism as Dialogue', 'Religion of No Religion', 'Wisdom of the Mountains', 'Transcending Duality' and 'Diamond Web', Public Lectures, Electronic University, Mill Valley, San Francisco, 1968-70

WORKS ON EASTERN
SPIRITUALISM BY
OTHER AUTHORS

Aitken, Robert, *Encouraging Words: Zen Buddhist Teachings for Western Students,* Pantheon, New York (USA), 1994

Baldock, John, *The Little Book of Zen Wisdom,* Vega, London (UK), 2002

Bayda, Ezra, Beck, Charlotte Joko, *Being Zen: Bringing Meditation to Life,* Shambhala, San Francisco (USA), 1996

Birx, Ellen, *Healing Zen: Awakening to Life of Wholeness and Compassion While Caring for Yourself and Others,* Viking, London (UK), 2002

Blackman, Sushila (ed.), *Graceful Exits: How Great Beings Die : Death Stories of Tibetan, Hindu & Zen Masters,* Weatherhill, London (UK), 1997

Dogen, Eihei, Steven Heine (transl.), *The Zen Poetry of Dogen: Verses from the Mountain of Eternal Peace.* Charles Tuttle, Boston (USA), 1997

Fletcher, Tenshin, Scott, David, *Way of Zen,* Vega, London (UK), 2002

Glassman, Bernard and Rick Fields, *Instructions to the Cook: A Zen Master's Lessons in Living a Life That Matters,* Random House, New York (USA), 1997

Haskel, Peter, *Bankei Zen: Translations from the Record of Bankei,* Grove Press, New York (USA), 1989

Karcher, Stephen, *I Ching,* Vega, London (UK), 2002

Kraft, Kenneth (ed.), *Zen: Tradition and Transition,* Grove Press, New York (USA), 1989

Kwok, Man-Ho, Palmer, Martin, Ramsey, Jay, *Illustrated Tao Te Ching,* Vega, London (UK), 2002

Lash, John, *The Yin of Tai-Chi: Tao, Tai-Chi and the Mysterious Female,* Vega, London (UK), 2002

Loori, John Daido, *Two Arrows Meeting in Mid-Air: The Zen Koan,* Charles Tuttle, Boston (USA), 1994

Marchaj, Konrad Ryushin, *The Heart of Being: Moral and Ethical Teachings of Zen Buddhism,* Charles Tuttle, Boston (USA), 1996

Matthiessen, Peter, *Nine-Headed Dragon River: Zen Journals 1969-1982,* Shambhala, San Francisco (USA), 1987

Miura, Isshu and Ruth Fuller Sasaki, *The Zen Koan,* Harcourt Brace, London (UK), 1989

Morgan Wood, Jan, *Easy-to-Use Shamanism,* Vega, London (UK), 2002

Nhat Hanh, Thich, *The Heart Of The Buddha's Teaching,* Parallax Press, London (UK), 1998

Roshi, Yasutani, Paul Jaffe (trans.), *Flowers Fall: A Commentary on Dogen's Genjokoan,* Shambhala, San Francisco (USA), 1996

Ryan, Robert E, *The Great Circle, Shamanism & the Psychology of C.G. Jung,* Vega, London (UK), 2002

Scott, David, *Easy-to-Use Zen,* Vega, London (UK), 2002

Shainberg, Lawrence, *Ambivalent Zen: A Memoir,* Pantheon, New York (USA), 1996

Shimano, Eido Tai, Kogetsu Tani (illus.), *Zen Word, Zen Calligraphy,* Shambhala, San Francisco (USA), 1995

St Ruth, Diana, St Ruth, Richard, *The Little Book of Buddhist Wisdom,* Vega, London (UK), 2002

Suzuki, Daisetz Teitaro, *An Introduction to Zen Buddhism* (foreword by C.G. Jung), Grove Press, London (UK), 1991

Uchiyama, Kosho, *From the Zen Kitchen to Enlightenment: Refining Your Life,* Weatherhill, London (UK), 1983

Victoria, Brian Daizen, *Zen at War,* Weatherhill, London (UK), 1997

Waddell, Norman, *The Essential Teachings of Zen Master Hakuin; A Translation of the Sikko-Roku Kaien-Fusetsu.* Shambhala, San Francisco (USA), 1994

INDEX

ZEN – THE SUPREME EXPERIENCE

We would like to thank the following for use of pictures:

CORBIS pp. 6, 8, 12, 22, 24, 27, 29, 30–31, 33, 35, 36–37, 39, 40, 43, 44–45, 47, 49, 52–53, 54, 57, 58–59, 61, 62, 65, 67, 68–69, 71, 72, 74–75, 76, 78, 80–81, 83, 85, 87, 88–89, 91, 92, 95, 96–97, 98, 101, 103, 104–105, 107, 109, 112–113, 114, 118–119, 121, 122–123, 125, 126, 127, 129, 132, 138, 140–141, 142, 145, 149, 151, 153, 154–155, 156, 158–159, 160, 163, 164–165, 167, 168, 170, 172–173, 174, 175, 177, 178–179, 180, 183, 184–185, 189, 190, 194, 196–197, 199, 200–201, 202, 204–205, 207, 209, 210, 212–213

TONY STONE IMAGES pp. 51, 110–111, 130–131, 136–137, 187

HUTCHINSON pp. 135, 147

ART ARCHIVE p. 192

PANOS p. 116

ACKNOWLEDGEMENTS